TAX Cafe™

Taxcafe.co.uk Tax Guides

Using a Property Company to Save Tax

By Carl Bayley BSc ACA

Important Legal Notices:

TAXCafe™
TAX GUIDE - 'Using a Property Company to Save Tax'

Published by:
Taxcafe UK Limited
214 High Street
Kirkcaldy KY1 1JT
Tel: (0044) 01592 560081
Email: team@taxcafe.co.uk

First Edition, February 2003
Second Edition, April 2003
Third Edition, January 2004
Fourth Edition, March 2004

ISBN 1 90608 14 0

Disclaimer

Before reading or relying on the content of this Tax Guide please read carefully the disclaimer on the last page which applies. If you have any queries then please contact the publisher at team@taxcafe.co.uk.

About the Author

Carl Bayley is the author of a number of tax guides designed specifically for the layman. Carl's particular speciality is his ability to take the weird, complex and inexplicable world of taxation and set it out in the kind of clear, straightforward language that taxpayers themselves can understand. As he often says, 'my job is to translate tax into English'.

Carl takes the same approach when speaking on taxation, a role he has undertaken with some relish on a number of occasions, including his highly acclaimed series of seminars at the Evening Standard Homebuyer Show.

In addition to being a recognised author and speaker on the subject, he has also spoken on property taxation on BBC radio and television.

A chartered accountant by training, Carl began his professional life in 1983, in the Birmingham office of one of the 'Big 4' accountancy firms. He qualified as a double prize-winner and immediately began specialising in taxation.

After 17 years honing his skills with major firms, Carl began the new millennium in January 2000 by launching his own Edinburgh-based tax consultancy practice, Bayley Consulting, through which he now provides advice on a wide variety of UK taxation issues, especially property taxation, Inheritance Tax planning and matters affecting small and medium-sized businesses.

As well as being Taxcafe.co.uk's Senior Consultant, Carl is also a director of accountancy firm Holmes & Bayley Limited, Chairman of the Institute Members in Scotland group and a member of the governing Council of the Institute of Chartered Accountants in England and Wales.

When he isn't working, Carl takes on the equally taxing challenges of hill walking and writing poetry.

Dedication

As usual, this book is dedicated to the two very special ladies who have shaped my life:

To Isabel, whose unflinching support has seen me through the best and the worst.

And to Diana, who made it all possible.

Thanks

Sincere thanks are also due to my good friend and colleague, Nick, who believed in me long before I did.

C.B., Edinburgh, March 2004

Contents

Foreword
By the author

People in the UK have invested in property for centuries. However, substantial increases in personal wealth and disposable income over the last few decades, together with recent difficulties in other areas of investment and in the pensions industry, have combined to make this an ever-increasingly important area of personal financial planning.

Despite the recent increase in interest rates and the media scrutiny of the self-certifying mortgage regime, I personally believe that the property investment sector as we know it today is here to stay. Naturally, the sector will have its ups and downs, as any other sector does, but the philosophy of property investment as a 'career move' is now so well entrenched that it is impossible to imagine that it could ever disappear altogether.

In March 2002, in response to the huge demand for advice on property taxation issues that we had been experiencing at Taxcafe.co.uk, we published the first edition of *How To Avoid Property Tax*, the sister publication to this guide. Since then, the demand for property taxation advice has continued to grow at a phenomenal pace and is responsible for the fact that our first guide is already in its sixth edition and this guide is now in its fourth.

But it isn't just the **quantity** of advice being demanded that we have seen increasing, it is also the level or, if you like, the **quality** of advice being demanded that we have seen increase significantly.

As I have already suggested above, a strong trend has now emerged for people to enter the property investment business as a profession. This 'new breed' of property investor is entering the market with a much higher degree of sophistication and is prepared to devote substantial time and resources to the business.

Almost every one of these 'professional investors' asks me the same question: "should I use a company?" Very often, they are hoping for a nice, simple, single-word answer and, being the helpful chap that I am, I give them one: "Maybe!"

Being an accountant, you may think that my slightly evasive response is merely a ploy to enable me to earn more fees from consultancy work. However, you would be quite wrong, as "maybe" is the only answer that I could possibly give. This question is not an easy one to answer. There are a huge number of factors to be taken into account, not all of which relate to taxation, and it is therefore impossible (not to mention inadvisable) to simply give a straightforward "yes" or "no". (And, in any case, I have plenty of consultancy work already, thank you!)

The aim of this guide, though, *is* to answer that question, not in a single word, but in the many thousands of words that in reality, the answer to this highly complex question actually requires.

So, to provide you with a truly thorough answer to this crucial question, we will begin by looking first in Chapters One and Two at the basic tax (and non-tax) implications of using a company. The UK tax regime for companies is quite different from that applying to individuals, or indeed to partnerships, trusts or other potential investment vehicles. The company tax regime has quite a few quirks, which can prove to be costly traps for the unwary. It is, therefore, extremely important that any property investor considering the company route understands what they are getting themselves into!

In Chapters Three to Eight we will move on to a more detailed look at the taxation of UK property companies. Here we will discover that there are several different types of property company and that each gives rise to a different set of tax implications that need to be considered carefully by the prospective corporate property investor.

Chapter Nine provides a summarised comparison of the tax position of companies and individuals. Following that, in Chapter Ten, we will take a detailed look at the factors involved in making the decision whether to use a company and their implications for the property investor. This is illustrated throughout by several examples designed to highlight the key issues involved.

Many more potential planning possibilities and possible pitfalls are picked up in Chapters Eleven to Fourteen, before we finally weigh the whole thing up in Chapter Fifteen at the end of the guide, where our detailed findings are neatly summarised.

Predicting the Future

In order to reinforce the issues discussed in this guide, I will demonstrate the tax implications of corporate property investment through the use of several worked examples. In my examples, I have naturally had to make various assumptions about external factors beyond the control of the property investor, including:

- The growth of property values
- The future rate of inflation
- Interest rates
- The rates of return on property investment
- Future changes to the UK tax system

I have made my assumptions as reasonable as possible based on my experience of the property investment sector and the UK taxation regime. However, if I can predict one thing with any certainty it is that the future will not be exactly as any of us may predict. Hence, while I still feel that the conclusions that I have been able to draw in this guide are validly based on sound principles, the reader must nevertheless bear in mind that those conclusions are, to some extent, dependent on uncertain predictions about the future.

Tips and Warnings

Sprinkled throughout the guide you will also find many 'Tax Tips' and 'Wealth Warnings' designed to highlight key points where there are extra savings to be made or traps to catch the unwary! Watch out for both of these as you read the guide.

In Conclusion

In the end, only **you** can really decide whether a property company is appropriate, by undertaking a detailed examination of your own individual position and weighing up all of the factors involved.

My aim in this guide is to enable you to reach that unique individual conclusion and make a well-informed decision armed with a strong understanding of the many factors involved.

By the way, although I referred earlier to 'professional investors', there are also quite a few 'gifted amateurs' around and the chances are that, if you've read this far into my introduction, you have a sufficiently professional approach to be considering using a company and therefore to benefit from this guide, regardless of how you came into property investment in the first place.

Finally, whatever type of property investor you are, and whatever decision you reach about the possible benefits of using a company, may I thank you for reading this guide and wish you every success with your investments.

Future Changes

This fourth edition of *Using a Property Company to Save Tax* incorporates all of the changes introduced by Gordon Brown's eighth Budget Statement on 17th March 2004, including the new measures relating to the payment of small company dividends.

However, amongst the many notices issued on 17th March was a statement that the tax position of small companies will be further reviewed later in the year. What such a further review might mean for property companies is difficult to judge at this stage, but in Chapter Sixteen at the end of the guide I have attempted to analyse the potential impact of further changes to small company taxation.

Nevertheless, despite the possibility of further changes to the tax regime for small companies, I remain firmly of the opinion that there will always still be a great many property investors for whom the use of a company vehicle to hold their investments will continue to be highly beneficial.

Chapter 1

Why Use a Company?

1.1 Introduction

Over the last few years, many UK property investors have been drawn towards the idea of holding their property investments through a limited company. Why is this?

Unlike most other types of business, it does not generally appear to be due to the perceived protection afforded by a company's limited liability status. In any case, limited liability status can now also be achieved through the medium of a Limited Liability Partnership (LLP), a new type of legal entity which was introduced to the UK in 2001.

No, this decision appears to be almost entirely tax-driven and is a direct result of the current highly favourable Corporation Tax regime.

Corporation Tax rates have been steadily falling over the last two decades. Finally, in April 2002, Gordon Brown shocked even the most veteran of professional Budget-watchers by announcing a new zero-rate tax band for companies. Many people have dubbed the new tax band a 'personal allowance for companies'.

For some property investors, the new zero-rate band has been seen as the final clincher. In their eyes they see this as final proof that using a company has to be the best option.

But is it really that simple? Clearly, the fact that we have published a whole guide dedicated to this question indicates that it is not!

Yes, at first glance, the Corporation Tax rates do look very attractive compared with Income Tax rates. However, as we will see, basing the decision to use a company on this one factor alone would be extremely short-sighted.

As we proceed to examine this issue in greater detail we will see that the Corporation Tax benefits will not always be as great as they may, at first, appear to be. A large part of the advantage gained through the lower Corporation Tax rates is often eliminated by the problems surrounding profit extraction. These problems have been further exacerbated by the introduction of a new regime for small company dividends with effect from 1st April 2004.

Furthermore, the greatest danger lies in the fact that the long-term position, taking capital growth and the eventual disposal of investment properties into account, may be significantly and detrimentally affected by the use of a company.

Nevertheless, despite the drawbacks mentioned above, there are still a great many situations where using a company can provide a very significant financial boost to the long-term property investor acquiring a portfolio of properties over time.

1.2 Why the Government Likes Companies

As already mentioned, Corporation Tax rates have been steadily falling in recent years and now stand at their lowest level for a very long time.

Why?

The official story is that the Government is concerned to keep the UK as a competitive business centre within the global economy.

And unofficially?

While the official reason given is undoubtedly a major factor in the Government's thinking, there is an additional 'unofficial' reason. Companies are subject to far more rules and regulations than individuals. Hence, the Government and its various institutions and departments have far more control over companies. This is useful for a number of purposes, including the ever-present need to police the so-called 'Black Economy' and fight tax evasion, money laundering and other criminal activities.

Hence, the Government has a very good reason to encourage businesses to form companies.

However, it does appear that just recently they have begun to get "cold feet" about just how much they have been encouraging small businesses to incorporate through the use of a beneficial Corporation Tax system. This has led to the withdrawal of the benefit of the Corporation Tax 'nil rate' band where profits are being distributed as dividends.

Nevertheless, whilst the Government has seen fit to withdraw a little bit of the incorporation tax "carrot", the company tax system still remains highly beneficial when compared with Income Tax year on year.

1.3 Non-tax Reasons for Using a Company

Before we go on to examine all of the taxation considerations behind the use of a company for property investment, it is first worth having a brief look at the non-taxation factors involved.

There are many non-taxation issues involved in the decision whether to use a company or not. Some of these are covered briefly below, although this list is far from exhaustive.

Limited Liability Protection

Although this does not appear to be the major reason behind most property investors' decision to incorporate, it is still, nevertheless, a factor to be considered.

A company is a separate legal entity and, as such, is responsible for its own debts and other liabilities.

The usefulness of this, however, is often limited. Banks, for example, will often insist on personal guarantees from the directors or shareholders before they will lend money to the company.

Furthermore, modern insolvency law passes a large part of the company's financial responsibilities to its directors, who may find themselves personally liable where the company has been used in an attempt to avoid the payment of liabilities arising in the course of its business.

Nevertheless, limited liability is useful when the business faces unexpected losses or legal liabilities. This will tend to be of particular relevance to those who are involved in property development, rather than pure property investment.

Status

A business that is run through a company is generally perceived as having more status than a business owned by an individual or a partnership. For some reason, everyone thinks that 'John Smith Investments Limited' sounds a lot more reliable than plain 'John Smith'. This perception is, of course, complete rubbish, as is evidenced by the many corporate collapses we have seen.

Nevertheless, the perception of companies as steady and reliable still remains and corporate property investors may find that they can use this to their advantage.

Flexibility of Ownership

Without the use of a company, it is difficult to involve many other people in the ownership of your property business. Joint ownership with your spouse is easy enough to achieve, but later, as the business hopefully grows, you may wish to involve adult children or key employees.

It is far easier to spread small parcels of ownership of the business through the medium of company shares.

Separation of Ownership and Management

A company structure will also enable you to separate ownership and management.

As your business grows and the years go by, you may eventually wish either to retire or to move on to other ventures. However, you may still have a highly profitable business that you do not wish to sell yet.

Using a company will enable you to retain ownership (as a shareholder) while passing management responsibility on to others (the directors). A company structure also enables this business succession process to take place at a more controlled and steady pace.

Tax Tip

Taking the succession planning idea a step further, a company is often a good tool for passing wealth on to your children (or other intended beneficiaries).

The problem with a property investment or letting business is that it does not qualify for Business Property Relief for Inheritance Tax purposes. Hence, on the owner's death, the whole portfolio is exposed to Inheritance Tax.

What a company can do in this situation is allow the owner to pass on small parcels of ownership over a number of years, thus making use of the Capital Gains Tax and Inheritance Tax annual exemptions and avoiding both taxes.

A sophisticated share structure will also enable you to keep control of your company while passing on a significant proportion of the underlying value to your children.

Finance

Many investors wishing to hold properties through the medium of a company find it difficult to obtain the level of finance which they require. This problem seems to most affect those who are just entering the buy-to-let market or who only have one or two existing investment properties. Typically, 70% seems to be the maximum Loan To Value (LTV) for the smaller corporate investor.

However, many more experienced brokers are able to assist the investor with this issue by putting them in contact with more sophisticated lenders that appreciate the fiscal advantages of a company and are therefore, shall we say, less suspicious of companies. The lesson here is 'shop around'.

Conversely, for the larger portfolio, corporate status seems to become a positive factor in the eyes of many lenders, probably for the reasons explained under 'Status' above.

Additionally, where the investor is non-UK resident, but looking to invest in the UK property market, the UK's lending institutions actually seem to favour the use of a UK registered company, as this gives the investor a presence in the UK.

Legal Rights

If you run your business through a company, you personally will no longer own property. Instead, you will own company shares. Legally, these are an entirely different kind of asset, giving rise to different legal rights.

What kind of difference this will make to your affairs will depend on your personal circumstances, as well as in what part of the UK (or other country) you and your properties are located.

As I am not a lawyer, I will not attempt to advise property investors on these issues, but the advice I will give is that you should get legal advice on the implications of owning your properties through a company.

Company Law

If you use a UK-registered company, you will be subject to the requirements of UK company law. This may restrict your ability to utilise funds from your business for private purposes (it is illegal for a company to lend money to its directors beyond certain rather restrictive limits).

Audit and Other Statutory Requirements

Larger companies require a statutory annual audit of their accounts. Broadly speaking, an audit will usually now only be required where the company meets two out of the following three criteria:

i)   Turnover exceeds £5,600,000 per annum.
ii)   Total asset value exceeds £2,800,000.
iii) The company has more than 50 employees.

Recent increases in the above limits have brought the UK into line with European Union directives on the subject, despite some opposition among the UK's major accountancy bodies.

Exceeding two of the above three limits makes an audit mandatory, but there is nothing to stop you having your company audited even if you do not meet these criteria. You might wish to do this, for example, if you have left the running of your company in the hands of managers and would like some independent verification of the company's financial results.

Even the smallest companies must file annual accounts, an annual return and certain other documentation with Companies House. As with taxation, there are penalties for late filing. For private companies, accounts must be filed within ten months of the accounting date. (Public companies, whether quoted on the Stock Exchange or not, have only seven months to file their accounts.)

Costs

Inevitably, the additional statutory requirements involved in running a company will lead to increases in accountancy and other professional costs. These additional costs must be weighed against the tax and other benefits that incorporation brings.

Time

Running a company will take up more of your time. There is more bureaucracy, more paperwork and more administration to think about. Whatever you do, there are only 24 hours in a day, so the time eaten up by bureaucracy means less time to concentrate on your investments. Hence, you have to ask yourself if the financial savings that the company brings are sufficient to compensate you for the time that the company takes up.

It's a question of how you value your time. If the company is saving you a large amount of money then obviously it is worth investing your time. But, in borderline cases, this could actually be the factor that decides against the company.

Naturally, if the company saves you enough money, it will be worth employing someone else to do all that tedious paperwork. Then you can save money and time!

1.4 Overview of Company Tax Pros & Cons

We now turn to the tax implications of running a property business through a company. As a broad overview, in general terms, it is reasonable to say that:

A company produces a better taxation result on <u>income</u>. BUT
Personal ownership produces a better result on <u>capital</u> growth.

To illustrate this further, let's take a look at some of the taxation pros and cons of investing through a limited company.

Using a Company: The Pros

Not CGT: IT on capital gains

- The first £10,000 of annual profit (or gains) retained in the company is tax free.

- Corporation Tax on any level of annual profits is charged at much lower rates than higher rate Income Tax.

- The maximum effective Corporation Tax rate on both profits and capital gains is 32.75%.

- Companies still get indexation relief for capital gains purposes. Indexation relief compensates you for that portion of your capital gain that is purely down to inflation.

- Stamp Duty is payable at a rate of only 0.5% on the purchase of company shares.

- You may choose any year-end accounting date for your company that you wish (an individual's property letting business must be accounted for on a tax year basis).

- Company shares may be passed on in small quantities at regular intervals, thus utilising the donor's Capital Gains Tax and Inheritance Tax annual exemptions.

- Losses arising from a company's property letting business may be set off against any other income the company has for the same period. (Individual property owners cannot do this.)

Using a Company: The Cons

- Companies do not get an annual exemption for capital gains purposes.

- Companies do not get taper relief for capital gains purposes. For individuals, trusts and partnerships, taper relief replaced indexation relief in 1998. Generally speaking, the longer you hold an asset, the more taper relief you get. This relief is covered more extensively later in the guide.

- Any personal use by the investor or his family of properties owned by the company may potentially have severe tax consequences. This should be contrasted with the Capital Gains Tax benefits of personal use when investing in property directly.

- Personal tax liabilities may arise when extracting trading or rental profits or property sale proceeds from the company.

- The company's Corporation Tax bill may also be increased when extracting profits or sale proceeds.

- It can sometimes be more difficult to obtain relief for certain administrative expenses, such as 'use of home as office' and motor expenses, when investing through a company.

- The new £1,500 Income Tax allowance for landlord's expenditure on loft and cavity wall insulation is not available to companies.

- There is no Stamp Duty exemption for lower value company share purchases (unlike the de minimis exemptions for lower value property purchases).

- Companies cannot have a Principal Private Residence, hence they are unable to claim the Principal Private Residence exemption, Private Letting Relief or Rent-A-Room Relief.

- UK resident companies face an 'exit charge' on emigration.

- Many other personal tax-planning techniques, such as investing in Enterprise Investment Scheme shares are simply not available to companies.

The reader will readily see that there are more cons than pros here, particularly when it comes to capital gains. Nevertheless, the benefits of the lower Corporation Tax rates are highly significant and will very often be large enough to ensure that the company route does remain preferable overall. This will become clear later on in the guide.

What all the 'cons' do mean, however, is that using a company is an extremely complex decision and requires some very careful consideration.

Chapter 2

A Plain English Guide to Corporation Tax

2.1 What Taxes do Companies Pay?

In this section, we will take a closer look at how Corporation Tax is calculated, not in the 'Tax Esperanto' favoured by many technical books on the subject, but in a more easily digestible format! First, it is worth summarising the different taxes that companies pay.

Income and Capital Gains

A UK resident company pays Corporation Tax on its worldwide income, profits and gains. It does not pay Income Tax or Capital Gains Tax. (You may have noticed in section 1.4, that I referred to 'capital gains' for companies, but not to 'Capital Gains Tax'.)

In arriving at its tax liability, a company's income and capital gains are simply aggregated together and then treated as a single total sum chargeable to Corporation Tax. The derivation of the actual amounts of rental profit, trading profit or capital gains on properties subject to Corporation Tax is explained further in Chapters Four and Five.

Generally speaking, capital gains, rental profits and trading profits are all calculated in much the same way as for private individuals. The differences arise in the way that the income and gains are taxed, the reliefs and exemptions available and the rates of tax applying. For capital gains, the biggest difference lies in the fact that companies continue to accumulate indexation relief on their capital assets but are not eligible for any form of taper relief.

We will return to the differences between the corporate and personal tax regimes again in Chapters Nine and Ten, where we will be taking a detailed look at their impact on the property investor.

Stamp Duty & Stamp Duty Land Tax

Companies pay Stamp Duty and Stamp Duty Land Tax on their purchases at exactly the same rates as an individual does. The only exception to this is that companies are now exempt from Stamp Duty on purchases of goodwill, although this will not often be relevant to property companies. (Stamp Duty and Stamp Duty Land Tax are covered further in Chapter Seven.)

Inheritance Tax

close companies.

Companies are only liable for Inheritance Tax in the most exceptional of circumstances and, even then, the tax only arises as a result of external factors involving the company's shareholders.

A company does not die, so Inheritance Tax does not arise. Instead, companies are wound up and we will come to the implications of this later in the guide. None of this, however, alters the fact that when a shareholder dies the value of his or her property company shares must be taken into account as part of the estate for Inheritance Tax purposes.

VAT

Broadly speaking, a company is liable for VAT in the same way as an individual (see Section 7.5).

National Insurance

If you employ anyone to help you in your corporate property business, the company will be liable for secondary Class 1 National Insurance Contributions, at the rate of 12.8%, in its capacity as an employer.

The company is also liable for Class 1A National Insurance Contributions on any benefits in kind provided to employees and Class 1B National Insurance Contributions on any voluntary settlements negotiated with the Inland Revenue (e.g. on the cost of sandwiches provided at lunchtime business meetings).

In this respect, there is no difference from the situation where you employ someone to help you in your business.

The key difference, however, comes from the fact that National Insurance will also be due if you pay yourself a salary out of the company's profits or provide yourself with any benefits in kind (such as a company car). We will look further at the implications of this in section 8.2.

Apart from secondary Class 1, Class 1A and Class 1B, however, a company cannot be liable for any other Class of National Insurance Contributions.

2.2 Corporation Tax in Plain English

Officially, there are three rates of Corporation Tax, the 'Starting Rate', the 'Small Companies Rate' and the 'Main Rate'. Currently, these are nil, 19% and 30% respectively.

However, the Corporation Tax system does not operate in the same way as the Income Tax system. A large company, paying tax at the main rate, does not benefit at all from the Starting Rate or the Small Companies Rate and will pay Corporation Tax at the main rate on all of its profits.

The benefit of the Starting Rate and the Small Companies Rate are progressively withdrawn through a system of marginal reliefs. From 1st April 2004, the benefit of the Starting Rate is also withdrawn from that part of a company's profits paid out as dividends. We will examine this situation in greater detail in section 2.3.

As a result of the marginal relief system, whilst there are only three official Corporation Tax rates, there are, in fact, no fewer than <u>five effective rates</u>.

The current effective Corporation Tax rates applying to profits arising on or after 1st April 2002 are given below. The rates applying for the two previous financial years (i.e. from 1st April 2000 to 31st March 2002) are given in brackets.

Corporation Tax Rates
On the Company's <u>Total Profits and Gains:</u>

First £10,000:	Tax free	(10%)
Next £40,000:		
(i.e. from £10,000 to £50,000)	23.75%	(22.5%)
Next £250,000:		
(i.e. from £50,000 to £300,000)	19%	(20%)
Next £1.2m:		
(i.e. from £300,000 to £1.5M)	32.75%	(32.5%)
Over £1.5m:	30%	(30%)

Example

Aaron Limited makes a total taxable profit of £400,000 for the year ended 31st December 2004. The company's Corporation Tax liability for the year can therefore be calculated as follows:

£10,000	*@*	*0%*	*=*	*£0*
£40,000	*@*	*23.75%*	*=*	*£9,500*
£250,000	*@*	*19%*	*=*	*£47,500*
£100,000	*@*	*32.75%*	*=*	*£32,750*
Total tax due:				*£89,750*

To simplify matters, however, it is worth noting that once a company's annual profit exceeds £50,000, the first two effective rates can simply be ignored and profits of up to £300,000 in total will be taxed at the single rate of 19% (20% before 1st April 2002).

Example Revisited

Let's look at Aaron Limited's Corporation Tax calculation again to see how this works in practice:

£300,000	@	19.00%	=	£57,000
£100,000	@	32.75%	=	£32,750
Total tax due:				£89,750

same

As can readily be seen, this much simpler calculation produces the same result.

Similarly, once the profits exceed £1,500,000, all profits are simply taxed at the main rate of 30% and the other four effective rates can all be ignored.

Note that when you receive a Corporation Tax calculation from the Inland Revenue (and perhaps also from your accountant), it will not look like either of the calculations in the example above. The Inland Revenue will follow the 'official' format using only the three official Corporation Tax rates mentioned above, with a deduction for marginal relief where applicable.

To see the calculation in the above example reproduced in the 'official' format turn to Appendix A at the back of this guide. For the remainder of the main body of the guide, however, we will stick with our unofficial format since it is by far the easier method to understand in practice and is also far more useful when we start to look at tax-planning issues.

Appendix A also covers the distortion to a company's Corporation Tax rates which can be caused if the company is in receipt of dividends from other UK companies.

Other complexities which sometimes arise in Corporation Tax calculations are covered in Appendix D, including the impact of changes in Corporation Tax rates during your company's accounting period and the effect of having an accounting period greater or shorter than a year in length.

2.3 The Impact of Dividends on Corporation Tax

From 1st April 2004, any part of the company's profit paid out as a dividend will no longer be eligible for the 'Starting Rate' of Corporation Tax (the 'nil rate'). This means that the effective rate of 23.75% applying to profits between £10,000 and £50,000 will also not apply.

In effect, any profits paid out as dividends will immediately be taxed at the 'Small Companies Rate' of 19%, regardless of the company's overall level of profit. The 32.75% marginal rate and the main rate of Corporation Tax are unaffected by this change.

Impact on Small Companies Paying Dividends

To illustrate the impact of this change, let's take a look at a short example.

Example

Hastings Limited makes a profit of £30,000 for Corporation Tax purposes for the year ended 31st March 2005. If none of this profit were paid out as a dividend, Hastings Limited's Corporation Tax bill would be:

£10,000 @ 0% =	£0
£20,000 @ 23.75% =	£4,750
Total	£4,750

Giving an overall effective Corporation Tax rate for Hastings Limited of 15.83%. However, during the year, Hastings Limited pays out dividends of £20,000. The company's Corporation Tax calculation is therefore now increased, as follows:

Profits distributed	
£20,000 @ 19% =	£3,800
Profits retained	
£10,000 @ 15.83% =	£1,583
Total	£5,383

There are a few important points to note here:

i) Terminology: The amount of profit paid out as a dividend is referred to as a 'distributed' profit.

ii) The amount not paid out is known as the 'retained' profit.

iii) In this case, the retained profit before tax is £10,000. The retained profit after tax is £4,617 (£10,000 LESS £5,383). Unless the company has distributable reserves brought forward from the previous period, the retained profit after tax must, under Company Law, always be positive. This serves to restrict the amount of dividends which may be paid and the impact of the new rules is to increase the effect of this restriction.

v-impt point.

iv) The average Corporation Tax rate arising under the original calculation is applied to the retained profit before tax.

v) A minimum rate of 19% is, however, applied to the distributed profit. In this case, this creates an additional tax cost of 3.17% on the amount distributed as a dividend. In other cases, the additional cost will be anything between 0% and 19%, depending on the level of the company's profits.

Impact on Small Companies Not Paying Dividends

The new rules do not affect any small companies that are not paying any dividends. This is a very important point and we will see the beneficial implications of this in more detail later in the guide.

Impact on Medium-Sized and Large Companies

The new rules will not have any impact on companies which are making an annual profit (before tax) of £50,000 or more. This is equally true whether these companies are paying any dividends or not.

Subsidiary Companies, etc

The new charge does not apply where the recipient of the dividend is itself another company. Hence, in the case of a wholly owned subsidiary, for example, the charge will have no effect.

2.4 Save Thousands in Tax with 'Marginal Rate' Planning

Accountants will often refer to a company's 'marginal' Corporation Tax rate. This is the effective Corporation Tax rate that applies to the top part of its income.

For example, a company with an annual profit of £400,000 has a marginal rate of 32.75% and a company with an annual profit of £20,000 has a marginal rate of 23.75%.

The lower marginal rate may be affected by the new rules regarding distributable profits, although it will remain relevant as long as at least some of the company's profits are being retained.

The importance of the marginal rate is that this is the effective tax rate applying to any additional income or profit and also the effective rate of tax relief available for any additional expenses or allowances (until the increase or decrease in profit takes the company into a different tax band altogether, in which case its marginal rate will have changed).

In other words, a company with a marginal Corporation Tax rate of 23.75% will pay 23.75 pence on each additional £1 of profit. Similarly, a company with a marginal Corporation Tax rate of 32.75% will obtain 32.75 pence worth of tax relief for every additional £1 of expense incurred or allowance claimed.

To illustrate the impact of marginal rates, let's return to Aaron Limited once more.

Example
As we know, the company's taxable profits of £400,000 give rise to a Corporation Tax liability of £89,750. However, let us suppose that this is before taking account of a capital allowances

claim on computer equipment that Aaron Limited bought for £20,000 on 31 December 2004. After claiming the capital allowances, (which are at 50% for any new plant and machinery bought by small businesses, as defined in the Companies Act, before 1 April 2005), the company's taxable profits will be reduced to £390,000 and its Corporation Tax computation will therefore now be as follows:

£300,000	*@*	*19.00%*	*=*	*£57,000*
£90,000	*@*	*32.75%*	*=*	*£29,475*

Total tax due:	*£86,475*

The tax saved is therefore £3,275 (£89,750 minus £86,475), which equates to 32.75%.

As we can see, the amount of tax saved by any additional claim or relief is based on the marginal rate and this is why this is such an important concept in tax planning.

Tax Tip

A company's marginal rate will often change from one year to the next. For example, Aaron Limited might be anticipating a fall in its profits (to below £300,000), such that its marginal rate for the following year would be reduced to 19%. In such a situation, a single day's delay in Aaron Limited's computer equipment purchase would have reduced the effective tax relief on this expenditure from £3,275 to £1,900. Hence, not only would the company have had to wait another year for its tax relief, it would also have been **£1,375 worse off!**

Accelerating tax relief is something most people will be familiar and comfortable with, even without the impact of a movement in marginal rates. However, consider this:

What if Aaron Limited had a marginal rate of 19% for the year ended 31 December 2004, but was anticipating an increase in profits for the following year, such that its marginal rate would increase to 32.75%? In this case, the company would be better off to *delay* the purchase of computer equipment until after its year end (i.e. until 1st January 2005).

Although this would mean postponing tax relief for this expenditure by a year, it would actually **save** the company an additional £1,375!

The impact of timing your business expenditure carefully will be at its most significant when considering a movement in the company's marginal rate of Corporation Tax from 0% to 23.75% (or vice versa).

2.5 Cash-flow Benefits of Using a Company

For most companies, payment of Corporation Tax is due in one single lump sum payable by the date falling nine months and one day after the end of the accounting period. *For example, the Corporation Tax for the year ended 31st December 2004 will be due by 1 October 2005.*

It is worth noting that the timing of a company's Corporation Tax payment is totally dependent on its accounting year-end date. This is quite different to individuals and partnerships, where tax is always due on the same dates under the Self Assessment system. (In other words, instalments on 31st January during the relevant tax year and 31st July following the relevant tax year, with a balancing payment, or sometimes a repayment, the following 31st January).

For stable property businesses, there is a huge cash-flow advantage to using a company. This is regardless, and quite independent, of any actual total tax savings, in absolute terms, that might also be involved. Let's look at an example by way of explanation:

Example
Lorraine has a thriving property business. Her Income Tax liability has remained at the same level for a number of years (pretty rare in practice, but this is just an example, after all) and hence she has to pay half her tax on 31st January within the year and half on the following 31st July. If we 'averaged out' these two payments, this would be equivalent, for cash-flow purposes, to a single payment on 1st May.

Remember that, like any other individual or partnership with property letting income, Lorraine MUST prepare her accounts to

5th April each year. Hence, she effectively has to pay her tax just **26 days** *after her accounting period!*

If we contrast the 26 day 'average' payment period with the nine months and a day available to companies, we can see what a large cash-flow advantage the companies have – over eight months!

Furthermore, if the Inland Revenue do indeed begin to collect tax on individuals' letting income through the PAYE system in some cases (as has been rumoured), the cash-flow advantage of using a company would be even greater.

Admittedly, at today's low interest rates, cash flow is perhaps not as important as it has been in the past. However, with interest rates beginning to creep up again, it may assume greater significance once more in the not too distant future. And, in any case, wouldn't you rather keep your money for an extra eight months? Think what you could do with it in that time, especially in the rapidly moving property investment sector!

What if Profit isn't Stable?

The example above is perhaps not entirely typical, as it is based on a stable annual profit. In practice, profits tend to be rising (one hopes), which means that the company cash-flow advantage is not quite so great. Nevertheless, in the vast majority of cases, the 'average' payment date for an individual investor (or a partnership) would still fall somewhere within three months of the accounting period, meaning that a company would usually produce at least six months of cash-flow advantage.

Wealth Warning

Note, however, that if the company is making large enough profits to be under the instalment system (see Appendix E), its 'average' payment date is actually about a month **before** the end of its accounting period. In this case, the company actually produces a cash-flow *disadvantage* (although, by the time profits have reached this kind of level, other considerations are likely to be far more important).

Tax Tip

As already explained, a company can choose any accounting year-end date that it wishes, whereas an individual property investor is forced to stick with 5th April.

In the corporate regime this can sometimes provide scope to delay the tax on profits which do not arise regularly over the year. This is particularly relevant to those letting furnished holiday accommodation or student accommodation.

Example

Laura lets out a number of student flats through a company, Laura's Lettings Limited. Generally, they are let from October to June, but are often vacant during the summer months. Hence, all of Laura's profit arises during the nine months to June. If the company were to draw up its accounts to 30th June each year, her Corporation Tax liability would be due on 1st April the following year. Instead of this, however, she arranges for Laura's Lettings Limited's accounting year-end to be 30th September. Her Corporation Tax liability is therefore not due until 1st July the following year. This one simple step has therefore given Laura an additional three-month cash-flow saving every year!

Chapter 3

The Different Types of Property Companies

3.1 Introduction

In Chapter 2 we looked at the basic mechanics of how a company is taxed in the UK. We will now begin looking in more detail at the specific UK taxation issues relating to *property* companies.

While it would be possible to come up with a very long list of different 'types' of property companies, I would tend to regard the following four categories as the definitive list as far as UK taxation treatment is concerned:

a) Property investment (or letting) companies
b) Property development companies
c) Property trading (or dealing) companies
d) Property management companies

Before we go on to look at the detailed tax treatment of these different types of property companies, it is perhaps worth spending a little time to explain exactly what these different terms mean in a taxation context.

I should probably also point out at this stage that there is nothing different about the way in which these different types of companies are formed, nor usually in their constitutions (see section 11.2). No, it is the nature of the property business itself that determines what type of company we are looking at.

It is also important to understand that these different types of property business are not exclusive to companies and that these different categorisations may also be applied to an individual property investor, a partnership, or any other kind of property investment vehicle.

The reason we need to consider these different types of property business here is the fact that an understanding of what type of property business you have is crucial in determining whether a company is appropriate for you.

Over the course of the next four chapters, we will examine the Corporation Tax consequences of having a company that falls into one of the four categories which I have outlined above, as well as the implications for the owner of the company. VAT and Stamp Duty Land Tax will then be considered in Chapter Seven.

National Insurance payable by companies was covered in section 2.1 and will be unaffected by the type of property business involved.

A company can, of course, carry on more than one type of property business, which would result in a mixture of tax treatments. I will spend a little time on the possible consequences of this in section 3.6.

3.2 Property Investment Companies (a.k.a. Property Letting Companies)

These are companies that predominantly hold properties as long-term investments. The properties are the company's fixed assets, which are held to produce income in the form of rental profit.

While capital growth will be anticipated and will form part of the company's business plan, property disposals should usually only take place where there is a strong commercial reason, such as an anticipated decline in value in that particular geographical location or a need to realise funds for other investments.

In general, properties will be held for a long period and rapid sales for short-term gain will be exceptional. Having said that, where unexpected opportunities for short-term gains do arise, it would be unreasonable to suggest that the company, like any other investor, should not make the most of them.

It is symptomatic of any property investment business (incorporated or not) that the investor has a minimal level of involvement in the day-to-day business. The majority of buy-to-let investors would, if investing through a company, be regarded as having this type of company.

Example
All Blacks Limited purchases three properties 'off-plan' in September 2004. On completion of the properties in January 2005, the company sells one of them in order to provide funds for continued expansion. The other two properties are then rented out for a number of years.

Although All Blacks Limited sold one of the properties very quickly, there was a good commercial reason for doing so. Hence, the company may be regarded as a property investment company.

Tax Treatment

A property investment company is <u>not</u> regarded as a trading company for tax purposes. This has some unfortunate consequences for the owner of the company, including:

i)   The shares in the company are not regarded as business assets for Capital Gains Tax taper relief purposes. Hence, only the slower 'non-business' rate of taper relief applies on a disposal of those shares (see further in Chapter Six).

ii)   The shares in the company are not eligible for Business Property Relief for Inheritance Tax purposes, meaning that the full value of the company would be included in the investor's estate on his death when calculating the Inheritance Tax due.

Tax Tip

Furnished holiday lettings (see section 4.5) enjoy a special status for tax purposes.

While companies whose income is derived mainly from these lettings continue to be regarded as property investment companies for a number of purposes, shares in such companies will remain eligible for 'business asset' taper relief. Shares in such companies will sometimes also be eligible for Business Property Relief for Inheritance Tax purposes.

A property investment company must account for its rental profits under the specific rules applying to income from land and property (see sections 4.1 to 4.6).

Property disposals are dealt with as capital gains.

Is there any advantage to being regarded as a property investment company rather than one of the other types of property company?

Very little!

The only advantage is the availability of indexation relief against capital gains. However, at the current low rate of inflation, this is of little benefit when compared with the loss of 'business asset' status on the company's shares for both Capital Gains Tax taper relief and Inheritance Tax purposes.

There is often, however, quite an advantage for an individual property investor (or a partnership, trust, etc.) in having a property investment business instead of one of the other types of property business. It is therefore important to understand what type of property business you have.

Although there is little advantage to this type of treatment, it is nevertheless important to remember that it is the way in which you carry on your business which determines the treatment, it is not a matter of choice!

As already stated, the vast majority of 'buy-to-let' investors are carrying on a property investment business and, hence, if they form a company, will have a property investment company.

This is, perhaps, unfortunate, since it is property investment businesses that produce the most uncertainty over whether the use of a company is beneficial or not.

For other types of property business, it is usually far more clear-cut that a company would be beneficial.

3.3 Property Development Companies

These are companies that predominantly acquire properties or land and carry out building or renovation work with a view to selling developed properties for profit.

The term covers quite a broad spectrum of activities, from major building companies that acquire vacant land and construct vast new property developments to small owner-managed companies that acquire the occasional 'run-down' property to 'do up' for onward sale at a profit. No one will doubt that the former are correctly categorised as property development companies, but not everyone realises that the latter type of activity will also lead to the company being regarded as a property development company.

Generally speaking, a property will be disposed of as soon as possible after building or renovation work has been completed. It is the profit derived from this work that produces the company's income and it does not usually look to rent properties out other than as a matter of short-term expediency.

Example
All Whites Limited purchases three old barns in February 2005 and converts them into residential property. The work is completed in August 2005 and the company sells two of the former barns immediately.

The third property, unfortunately, proves difficult to sell. In order to generate some income from the property, All Whites Limited lets it out on a short six-month lease. The property is never taken off the market during the period of the lease and a buyer is found in January 2006, with completion taking place in March.

Although All Whites Limited had let one of the properties out for a short period, its main business activity remained property development. This was reinforced by the fact that the property had remained on the market throughout the lease. All Whites Limited is therefore a property development company.

Tax Treatment

A property development company is regarded as a trading company. Shares in the company are therefore usually regarded as business assets for both Capital Gains Tax taper relief and Inheritance Tax purposes.

The company's profits from its property development activities, i.e. the profits arising from development property sales, are taxed as trading profits. (We will look at trading profits in more detail in section 4.8.)

Where, as in the example above, there is some incidental short-term rental income it should, strictly speaking, still be dealt with under the specific rules applying to income from land and property. In practice, however, it has sometimes been known for this to be accepted as incidental trading income.

Capital gains treatment will continue to apply to any disposals of the company's long-term fixed assets, such as its own offices, for example.

Larger property development businesses, which utilise the services of sub-contractors, are required to operate the Construction Industry Scheme for tax purposes. Broadly, this involves having to deduct tax, at a special rate particular to the Construction Industry Scheme, from payments made to sub-contractors and then account for it to the Inland Revenue, rather like PAYE.

3.4 Property Trading Companies

This type of company is fairly rare. Property trading companies are companies that generally only hold properties for short-term gain. Properties are bought and sold frequently and are held as trading stock. Such companies may sometimes also be known as property dealing companies.

Properties will not usually be rented out, except for short-term financial expediency.

The company's income is derived by making a profit on the properties it sells.

These companies differ from property development companies in that no actual development takes place on the properties. Profits are made simply by ensuring a good margin between buying price and selling price.

Example
All Greys Limited buys 20 properties 'off-plan' in March 2004. On completion of the development in October 2004, it sells all 20 properties at a considerable profit.

Since All Greys Limited has neither developed the properties, nor held on to them as investments for any length of time, it is clearly a property trading company.

Tax Treatment

A property trading company's profits should be taxed as trading profits (see section 4.8).

As with a property development company, any incidental letting income that does arise should be dealt with under the specific rules applying to income from land and property.

Shares in such a company are specifically not eligible for Business Property Relief for Inheritance Tax purposes.

As for Capital Gains Tax taper relief, the theory is that a property trading company is still a 'trading company' and hence the shares in such a company should be eligible for the faster 'business asset' taper relief. In practice, however, I feel that there is a strong danger that some resistance will be encountered, with the Inland Revenue contending that the company is, in fact, a property investment company and hence its shares do not qualify as 'business assets'. Time will tell on this one!

Wealth Warning

The major difference between property investment and property trading lies in the treatment of the profit arising on property disposals. In essence, the question is whether such 'profits' are capital gains or trading profits.

This is very much a 'grey area' and hence the Inland Revenue can be expected to examine borderline cases very carefully and to argue for the treatment that produces the most tax.

As explained above, the Inland Revenue may be inclined to deny the existence of a trading activity where taper relief is at stake.

Conversely, where an investor is potentially exempt from Capital Gains Tax (e.g. a non-resident) on capital gains, the Inland Revenue may argue that there is a trading activity in order to be able to levy Income Tax on that investor instead. (Assuming that we are talking about a UK property business.)

A company vehicle may be useful in this latter case, as there is less difference in the amount of tax payable *within* a company between a property 'trading' business or a property 'investment' business. Although this does effectively mean 'admitting defeat' and accepting that the business will be taxable in the UK, it is nevertheless a case of 'damage limitation' as the Corporation Tax rates applying will generally be lower than the Income Tax which is potentially at stake.

3.5 Property Management Companies

These companies do not generally own properties at all. Instead, they provide management services to property owners. If you have a property letting agent taking care of the day-to-day running of your properties, the chances are that it is probably a property management company. However, the interesting tax-planning point is that you can set up your own property management company!

A property management company's income is derived from the management or service charges it charges to the actual owners of the property.

Tax Treatment

A property management company is a trading company for all tax purposes.

Hence, shares in such a company are usually regarded as business assets for both Capital Gains Tax taper relief and Inheritance Tax purposes.

The company's profits from its property management activities will be treated as trading profits.

Any incidental letting income should, as usual, be dealt with under the specific rules applying to income from land and property.

The possible use of such a company for tax-planning purposes is covered later, in section 14.5.

3.6 Companies With a 'Mixed' Property Business

"What if my company doesn't happen to fit neatly into one of these four categories?" you may be asking.

If the company has a 'mixed' property business, involving more than one of the four types of property business described above, to a degree that is more than merely incidental, then, for Corporation Tax purposes, each of the business types will be dealt with separately, in the usual manner applicable to that type. It may even be necessary to draw up separate accounts for the different elements of the business.

The impact on the owner of the company may not necessarily be so straightforward.

Impact on Taper Relief

For Capital Gains Tax taper relief purposes, the company will only be considered to be a trading company (and hence its shares be eligible to be treated as 'business assets'), if its activities do not include any 'substantial' element of non-trading activities. For this purpose, property investment and property letting are deemed to be non-trading activities (except furnished holiday lettings, as previously explained).

The Inland Revenue has very helpfully told us that they will regard 'substantial' as meaning 'more than 20%'. "More than 20% of what?" you ask. Here, they have retained a little more control over the situation since, depending on the facts of the case, they may apply this '20% rule' to any of the following:

- Turnover (i.e. gross income)

- Expenditure

- Time spent by directors and employees

- Asset values

Wealth Warning

As explained in further detail in Chapter Six, whether your company shares qualify as 'business assets' for Capital Gains Tax purposes can make an enormous difference to the amount of tax you will pay on a sale of those shares or a winding up of your company.

Potentially, by allowing your shares to become 'non-business assets' for this purpose you could be increasing your Capital Gains Tax bill by a factor of four!

Tax Tip

To preserve the 'business asset' status of company shares, it will often be worth keeping any deemed 'non-trading' activities separate from those activities that are accepted by the Inland Revenue as having trading status. This can be done either by keeping the 'non-trading' activities out of the company, or by putting them into a different company. The possible benefits of multiple companies are examined further in section 14.4.

Impact on Business Property Relief for Inheritance Tax

The test for whether shares in a company with a 'mixed' property business qualify for Business Property Relief is considerably less stringent than the taper relief test above.

It is only necessary to ensure that the company's business does not consist wholly or mainly of property investment, property letting or dealing in property.

'Mainly' is defined as 50%, meaning that a property company's shares will be eligible to be treated as 'business assets' for Inheritance Tax purposes as long as over half of its business comes from property development or property management.

Chapter 4

Property Income & Expenses

4.1 Corporation Tax on Rental Profits

From a purely accounting point of view, property letting is treated like any other business for Corporation Tax purposes. The company has to draw up accounts, usually on an annual basis, which detail all of its rental (or other) income, as well as all relevant expenses.

The company must always produce one single set of accounts, detailing all of its activities, which it must file at Companies House.

Generally speaking, this one single set of accounts will usually also be sufficient for Corporation Tax purposes. If the company is letting a number of UK properties on a commercial basis, these will be treated as a single UK property business. Landlords operating through companies may, of course, draw up separate sets of management accounts for any individual property, or group of properties, if they wish.

Some types of letting must, however, be accounted for separately for Corporation Tax purposes, as they are subject to different tax rules. In these cases, a separate set of accounts will be required in support of the company's Corporation Tax calculations. These separate accounts do not, however, need to be filed with Companies House.

Separate letting accounts are required in the following cases:

- Overseas lettings.

- Non-commercial lettings.

Separate accounts may also be advisable in the case of any 'furnished holiday lettings' (see section 4.5) in order to safeguard the additional taxation benefits attaching to such lettings.

'Non-commercial lettings' refers to cases where less than full market rent is charged for a property due to some special relationship between the landlord and the tenant. Generally, as we will see later in the guide, I would advise strongly against holding such properties through a company.

In tax jargon, UK letting income, as well as most other non-trading income from UK land and property is referred to as 'Schedule A income'. Income from overseas property falls under 'Schedule D Case V', which is tax jargon for foreign income.

Company accounts must be drawn up in accordance with UK GAAP. Avoiding accountancy jargon, this means 'Generally Accepted Accounting Principles'. From 1st January 2005, it will also be permissible to use International Accounting Standards (IAS) and, in fact, large companies will actually be required to use these. For the vast majority of small or medium-sized property companies, however, there is no practical difference between the two methods.

The most important aspect of Generally Accepted Accounting Principles (or International Accounting Standards) is that accounts must be drawn up on an 'accruals' basis. This means that income and expenditure is recognised when it arises, or is incurred, rather than when it is received or paid (the latter being the 'cash basis', which is not permitted for Corporation Tax purposes).

Example
Jake and Sandy own a small property company, Braun Properties Limited, which draws up accounts to 30th November

each year. Braun Properties Limited acquires a new property on Kirkcaldy High Street in October 2004 and rents it out for the first time on 29th November at a monthly rent of £1,000 payable in advance.

At 30th November 2004, Braun Properties Limited will have received one monthly rental of £1,000. However, under the 'accruals' concept, Braun Properties Limited is only required to account for income of £66 (£1,000 x 12 x 2/365 – i.e. two days' rent) in its 2004 accounts. This simple (and correct) adjustment could reduce Braun Properties Limited's Corporation Tax bill on 1st September 2005 by up to £306.

Tax Tip

Expenses should similarly be recognised as they are incurred. The timing of allowable expenditure is therefore critical in planning your Corporation Tax affairs and it is the date that expenses are *incurred* (i.e. when work takes place, or goods are purchased) that is important, not when they are invoiced or paid for.

Example

Aileen has a company with an accounting date of 31st March, and has some roof repairs carried out on one of the company's rented properties in March 2004.

The roofer does not get around to invoicing Aileen's company until May and she pays him in July.

Despite the fact that Aileen does not pay for the repairs until July, she may nevertheless still deduct the cost in her company accounts for the year ended 31st March 2004.

4.2 Expenses You Can Claim

The rules on what types of expenditure may be claimed as deductions are much the same as for property-letting businesses run by individuals or partnerships.

Some of the main deductions include:

- Interest and other finance costs (see Chapter Thirteen for associated tax-planning issues)

- Property maintenance and repair costs

- Heating and lighting costs, if borne by the landlord company

- Insurance costs

- Letting agent's fees

- Advertising for tenants

- Accountancy fees

- Legal and professional fees (see further below)

- The cost of cleaners, gardeners, etc, where relevant

- Ground rent, service charges, etc.

- Bad debts

- Pre-trading expenditure (see further below)

- Administrative expenditure (see further below)

- Salaries paid to staff or directors (the latter is covered in more detail in section 8.2)

All expenses must be incurred wholly and exclusively for the purposes of the company's business and, naturally, must actually be borne by the company itself (i.e. the company cannot claim any expenses if the tenant is paying them directly).

Legal and Professional Fees

Legal fees and other professional costs incurred for the purposes of the business may be claimed as a deduction against rental income. Typically, this will include items such as the costs of preparing tenants' leases and, perhaps, debt collection expenses.

Legal fees and other costs incurred on the purchase or sale of properties, however, may not be claimed against rental income. All is not lost though, as these items may be claimed as allowable deductions for capital gains purposes (see Chapter Five).

Pre-trading Expenditure

You may incur some expenses for the purposes of your property business before you form your company or start to let out any properties.

In general, deductible expenses incurred within seven years before the commencement of a business may still be allowable if they would otherwise qualify under normal principles. In such cases, the expenses can be claimed as if they were incurred on the first day of the business.

Tax Tip

In the case of a new company, a number of 'pre-trading' expenses will often have been paid for by the investor personally before the company has been formed.

The best thing to do in these circumstances is to:

i) Keep track of the relevant expenditure, retaining receipts, etc, as usual.

ii) Once the company has been formed, 'recharge' the expenses to the company. What this means in practice is that a 'director's loan account' is set up in the company recording the expenditure previously incurred by the director.

iii) The expenses recharged by the director may (subject to the normal principles of deductibility) be claimed in the company's first accounting period.

iv)   The director may be repaid the 'loan account' as soon as the company has available funds.

Administrative Expenditure

This heading is perhaps the broadest, and can extend to the cost of running an office, motor and travel costs.

In the case of a company, it will also cover costs associated with running the company itself, (as opposed to running its business). This would include filing fees payable to Companies House and audit fees, if applicable. Costs of the company formation (see section 11.1) are not allowable as these are deemed to be a capital item.

As usual, the rule is that any expenditure must be incurred wholly and exclusively for the purposes of the business. Unfortunately though, business entertaining expenditure is specifically excluded. (Staff entertaining is allowed though – and will not even give rise to Income Tax charges unless the Inland Revenue's prescribed limits are exceeded.)

4.3 Capital Spending You Can Claim

The main types of disallowable expenditure in a property-letting or property-investment business are capital expenditure on property improvements and on furniture, fixtures and fittings. There are special rules for capital expenditure, depending on the type of property being rented:

a) So-called 'industrial property' attracts capital allowances on the cost of the building itself. These allowances are at the rate of 4% of cost per annum, but usually only apply to large structures, such as factories and warehouses, although they can also extend to garage workshops, for example.

b) Other commercial property, such as shops, offices etc, do not attract any allowances on the structure. However, any fixtures and fittings provided by the landlord in non-residential property do attract allowances. These allowances are more generous, up to 50% of cost being allowed in the first year (depending on the size of your business – see below) and 25% per annum of the unrelieved balance thereafter.

c) Residential property does not usually attract any capital allowances at all. However, landlords may claim a 'wear and tear allowance' (see section 4.4) on furnished lettings.

d) Furnished holiday lettings (see section 4.5), however, are not eligible for the wear and tear allowance, but are eligible for capital allowances in the same way as (b) above.

Capital allowances claimed previously may be reclaimed by the Inland Revenue, i.e. added back on to income (known as a 'balancing charge') when the property is sold.

The allowance of up to 50% under (b) above is only available for small companies incurring capital expenditure during the one year period from 1st April 2004 to 31st March 2005. From 1st April 2005, this rate will revert to 40%, in line with that available for "medium-sized" companies.

"Small" and "Medium-Sized" for these purposes are as defined under Company Law. Broadly speaking, a company is "Small" if it meets at least two of the following three tests:

i) Turnover (i.e. gross income) does not exceed £5,600,000 per annum.
ii) Total asset value does not exceed £2,800,000.
iii) It has no more than 50 employees.

Most property companies will tend to qualify as "Small" on the basis that they meet tests (i) and (iii).

A "Medium-Sized" company is one which fails to meet the "Small" company test, but which does meet at least two out of the following three tests:

i) Turnover (i.e. gross income) does not exceed £22,800,000 per annum.
ii) Total asset value does not exceed £11,400,000.
iii) It has no more than 250 employees.

Insulation Costs

From 6th April 2004, individual landlords will be able to claim an Income Tax deduction for up to £1,500 of expenditure on new loft or cavity wall insulation in residential properties. Unfortunately, however, this deduction is not available for Corporation Tax purposes and companies incurring such expenditure will have to continue to treat is a capital item.

4.4 Furnished Lettings

Income from furnished lettings (other than furnished holiday lettings, as defined – see section 4.5) is treated in much the same way as other rental income. The only differences, quite naturally, being related to the treatment of the furnishings.

No allowance is given for the initial expenditure in furnishing the property. Thereafter, the landlord company may claim either:

a) Renewal and replacement expenditure, or

b) The "wear and tear allowance"

The Wear & Tear Allowance

A "Wear and Tear Allowance" of 10% of net rents receivable may be claimed against the rental income from furnished residential lettings. This Allowance is given instead of Capital Allowances, which are not available, and as an alternative to the "Replacements Basis".

In calculating the Allowance, we first need to establish the amount of "net rents receivable" for the property in question.

"Net rents receivable" means the total rent receivable less any amounts borne by the landlord which would normally be a tenant's own responsibility (e.g. council tax, water rates or electricity charges).

Additionally, if the rental includes any material amount representing a payment for additional services which would normally be borne by the occupier, rather than the owner, of the property, then these amounts must also be deducted before calculating the 10% Allowance.

Example

Carling Limited owns a large flat in Twickenham, which is let out for £2,500 per month (£30,000 per annum). This includes a charge of £250 per month for the provision of a cleaner. Carling Limited also pays the water rates for the property, which amount to £1,000 per year, but the tenants pay their own council tax.

Carling Limited is therefore able to claim a wear and tear allowance as follows:

Total Rent Received:	*£30,000*
Less:	
Cleaning charges:	*£3,000 (12 x £250)*
Water Rates	*£1,000*
Net rent receivable:	*£26,000*
Wear and Tear Allowance:	*£2,600 (10%)*

Note that whilst we only have to deduct the COST of the water rates, it is the amount which Carling Limited CHARGES for the provision of cleaning services which must be deducted in this calculation. (Although only the cost thereof can be deducted when arriving at the company's overall total rental profits.)

The Alternative: The "Replacements Basis"

The Wear and Tear Allowance is not mandatory. Landlords may, instead, claim the cost of repairing, replacing or renewing furniture and fixtures. They may not, however, claim the costs of the original furnishings and fixtures when the property is first let out, nor the cost of improvements or additional items.

For example, replacing one Video Recorder with another (lucky tenants!) would be allowed under the Replacements Basis, but replacing a Video Recorder with a DVD Player (even luckier tenants!) would not, as it would represent an improvement.

The "Catch"

The Wear and Tear Allowance and the Replacements Basis are alternatives. You may claim one OR the other, NOT both.

However, building repair costs continue to be allowable under both methods and this extends to repairs and replacements of any items normally provided in an unfurnished property, such as sinks or toilets, for example

The "BIG" Catch

Once you have chosen one method, you must stick with it, on ALL of your furnished lets of all properties!

Hence, once the wear and tear allowance has been claimed, no deductions can ever be claimed for any repairs or renewals of furniture, fixtures, etc.

Tax Tip

If you were considering acquiring two or more properties and did have a clear idea that the wear and tear allowance was best for one (or more) of them, but the replacements basis would be better for the rest, you could consider acquiring the "wear and tear" properties personally, whilst you could use a company to acquire the others and elect for the replacements basis. (Or vice versa.)

This is permissible since you and your company are considered to be different persons for tax purposes.

So, Which Method Is Best?

Conventional wisdom states that the Wear and Tear Allowance is usually best. This is generally because this method provides some relief immediately, from the first year onwards.

Generally, it will take longer before replacement expenditure starts to come through, with the original capital cost of furnishings being unallowable.

In short, Wear and Tear generally provides faster relief.

However, it is worth bearing in mind that this will not always be the case.

Example 2

Beaumont Limited rents out a number of small flats to students at the local Polytechnic (sorry, it's called a UNIVERSITY now).

Bill (who owns Beaumont Limited) is constantly frustrated by the fact that the company's student tenants frequently wreck the furniture. However, he combats this by buying cheap furniture and keeping their security deposits.

As a result, Beaumont Limited's total rental income for 2004/2005 is £20,000. Out of this the company has paid Council Tax and Water Rates totaling £2,000 and spent £3,000 on replacement furniture.

If Beaumont Limited were to claim the Wear and Tear Allowance, it would only be able to deduct £1,800 from its rental income. Hence, in this case, the company is much better off claiming £3,000 under the Replacement Basis.

(With apologies to all those students who treat their landlord's property with the utmost respect and to any student landlords who do not buy cheap furniture or look for any excuse to hang on to their security deposits.)

So How Do You Choose?

Despite the example of Beaumont Limited, most property investment companies will be better off with the Wear and Tear Allowance. However, before you submit your first claim, I would suggest you do a few quick calculations to see which method is likely to be better for you on average in the long run (and not just in the first year).

4.5 Furnished Holiday Lettings

UK properties qualifying as 'furnished holiday lettings' enjoy a special tax regime, with many of the tax advantages usually only accorded to a trade.

The benefits for a shareholder owning a company which is mainly engaged in furnished holiday lettings were considered in section 3.2.

It is now worth us taking a brief look at the qualification requirements for a 'furnished holiday letting':

i) The property must be situated in the UK (this excludes the Channel Islands and the Isle of Man).

ii) The property must be furnished. As with other furnished lettings, however, there is no stipulation regarding the standard to which it must be furnished. In practice, it would come down to a question of whether a reasonable person would regard the property as 'furnished'. (In commercial terms, it would probably be quite impractical to attempt to meet the further requirements set out at (iii) to (vi) below without a suitable level of furnishing.)

iii) It must be let out on a commercial basis with a view to the realisation of profits.

iv) It must be available for commercial letting to the public generally for at least 140 days in a 12-month period.

v) It must be so let for at least 70 such days.

vi) The property must not normally be in the same occupation for more than 31 consecutive days at any time during a period of at least seven months out of the same 12-month period as that referred to in (iii) above.

The 12-month period referred to in (iv) and (vi) above is normally the twelve months ending on the last day of the relevant accounting period, but special rules apply for the years in which letting commences or ceases. A system of averaging may be used to determine whether a company with more than one property meets (v) above. This requires a claim by the company.

4.6 Tax Treatment of Rental Losses

UK Property Lettings

Subject to the exception set out below, for Corporation Tax purposes all of a company's UK property lettings are treated as a single UK property business. Hence, the loss on any one such property is automatically set off against profits on other commercially let UK properties for the same period.

Any overall net losses arising from a company's UK property-letting business will be set off against the company's other income for the same period (if any). Any remaining surplus loss is carried forward and set off against the company's total profits for the next accounting period, then the next, and so on. Rental losses may be carried forward for as long as is necessary in this way, provided that the company is still carrying on a UK property-letting business in the accounting period for which the claim to offset the losses is made.

Example
Namibian Underdogs Limited has a UK property-letting business, as well as a steady income of £10,000 each year in interest.

Unfortunately, in the year ended 31st December 2003, the company incurs a loss of £50,000 in its letting business.

£10,000 of the loss is therefore set off against the company's interest income for the year and the remaining £40,000 is carried forward.

In the year ended 31st December 2004, Namibian Underdogs Limited makes a profit of £8,000 on its property letting business.

The brought forward loss of £40,000 is treated as a letting loss for the year, resulting in an overall net loss on the letting business for Corporation Tax purposes this year of £32,000. As before, £10,000 of this is set off against the other income of the period, leaving a loss of £22,000 to carry forward.

In the year ended 31ˢᵗ December 2005, the company makes a final profit of £3,000 from UK property letting before deciding to give this business up.

The brought forward loss of £22,000 is again treated as a letting loss for the year, resulting in an overall net loss on the letting business for Corporation Tax purposes in 2005 of £19,000. Once again, £10,000 of this is set off against the interest income for the period. The remaining unrelieved loss of £9,000 may not, however, be carried forward, as the UK letting business has now ceased. This loss is therefore effectively 'wasted'.

It is worth noting in the above example that the surplus letting losses are set off against the company's other income even though it might, in fact, have had no Corporation Tax to pay on the first £10,000 of annual profits. Hence, quite a lot of the letting loss may actually have been 'wasted', not just the final 'unrelieved' portion.

Wealth Warning

It should be noted that rental losses incurred in a company can only be set off against the company's income of the same or future periods.

There is no scope for setting such losses off against any rental profits which the owner of the company may have as an individual.

Overseas Lettings

All of a company's commercial overseas lettings are treated as a single business for Corporation Tax purposes. This is treated as a separate business to the company's UK property letting business (if any).

Any loss on this business may be carried forward and set off against future profits from the same business – i.e. against future overseas rental profits received by the company.

Exception: Uncommercial Lettings

Any losses arising on lettings which are not entered into on a commercial basis are not available for any form of Corporation Tax relief. This applies equally whether the property concerned is in the UK or overseas.

Example
Gibbs Limited owns a flat in Cardiff which it lets out to Scott, the 79-year-old father of the company's owner. Scott only pays £100 a month in rent for the flat, despite the fact that the market rent for the property would be about £400 a month.

As a result, Gibbs Limited makes a substantial loss on this property. This loss cannot be relieved for Corporation Tax purposes.

There are two further important points which I need to make here:

i)   If Gibbs Limited made a profit on this property, it would still be taxable.

ii)   This situation would give rise to a great many problems for Gibbs Limited and for Scott's son, the owner. These are examined further in section 14.2.

4.7 Other Property Income

Any form of income, profit or gains derived from property which the company receives will generally be subject to Corporation Tax.

Lease Premiums

Lease premiums have a particularly complex treatment for Corporation Tax purposes.

4.7.1 Granting A Short Lease

Premiums received for the granting of short leases of no more than 50 years' duration are treated as being partly income derived from land and property and partly capital disposal proceeds, potentially giving rise to a capital gain.

The proportion of the premium treated as capital disposal proceeds is equal to 2% of the total premium received for each full year of the lease's duration in excess of one year. The capital gain arising is calculated on the basis of a part disposal of the relevant property.

The remainder of the premium is treated as rental income.

Example
Telstra Limited owns the freehold to a property. The company grants a 12-year lease to Fiji Limited for a premium of £50,000.

The lease exceeds one year by 11 years and hence 22% of this sum (£11,000) falls within the capital gains regime. This will be treated as a part disposal of the property and may or may not give rise to a taxable capital gain for Telstra Limited.

What is certain, however, is that Telstra Limited will be subject to Corporation Tax on deemed rental income of £39,000 (i.e. £50,000 less 22%).

4.7.2 Granting A Long Lease

The grant of a lease of more than 50 years' duration is treated purely as a capital disposal. The Base Cost (see section 5.3) to be used has to be restricted under the "part disposal" rules. In essence, what this means is that the Base Cost is divided between the part disposed of (i.e. the lease) and the part retained (the "reversionary interest") in proportion to their relative values.

Example

JPR Limited owns the freehold of a commercial property in Llanelly. The company grants a 60-years lease to Brian, a businessman from Belfast moving into the area. Brian pays a premium of £90,000 for the lease. The value of JPR Limited's reversionary interest is established as £10,000.

The Base Cost to be used in calculating JPR Limited's capital gain on the grant of the lease is therefore 90% of its Base Cost for the property as a whole.

4.7.3 Assigning a long lease with no less than 50 years' duration remaining

This is simply a straightforward capital disposal. Any applicable reliefs may be claimed in the usual way.

4.7.4 Assigning a short lease with less than 50 years' duration remaining

This is treated entirely as a capital disposal. However, leases with less than 50 years' remaining are treated as "wasting assets". The company is therefore required to reduce its Base Cost in accordance with a schedule contained in tax legislation. For example, for a lease with 20 years' remaining, and which had more than 50 years' remaining when first acquired, the Base Cost must be reduced to 72.77% of the original amount.

4.8 How Property Trading Profits are Taxed

As explained in Chapter Three, some property companies are not taxed under the rules for rental profits, as set out in sections 4.1 to 4.6, but are, instead, taxed on the basis that all the income from their property business represents trading profit. In tax jargon, trading profits are referred to as 'Schedule D Case I' income.

The most important differences in being a 'trading company' are probably the implications for the owner and these have already been dealt with in Chapter Three. As far as the computation of profits is concerned, the differences are not huge and there is therefore little point in repeating all of the rules from scratch once more.

What I will do in this section, therefore, is consider the differences between the taxation of trading profits and rental profits. These can be summarised as follows:

i) In the case of property development or property trading, the disposal proceeds received on the sale of a property represent trading income. Likewise, the cost of properties acquired represent 'cost of sales' and may be deducted from sale proceeds at the time of the property's sale.

ii)   Legal and professional fees and other costs incurred on the purchase or sale of properties may be claimed as trading expenses.

iii)   The wear and tear allowance (see section 4.4) is not applicable in a trading profits computation.

iv)   Capital allowances may only be claimed in respect of assets acquired as long-term fixed assets of the business. Where capital allowances are claimed, however, the relevant assets are 'pooled' together (except for motor cars, which are subject to restrictions on the amount of capital allowances available). The effect of the 'pooling' basis for assets other than motor cars is that balancing charges will not arise simply because one particular asset has been disposed of.

v)   The cost of any furnishings purchased and sold with a property may be deducted as 'cost of sales' against the disposal proceeds from that property.

vi)   All of the company's business will usually be treated as a single business, regardless of where its properties are located. This will all be treated as UK trading income if the business is all <u>run</u> from the UK.

vii)   Trading losses may be set off against the company's other income *and capital gains* of the same accounting period. Unlike rental losses, however, the company is not forced to make this set-off and may choose not to claim it. (This may be desirable if, for example, the company's other income for the period falls wholly within the nil rate Corporation Tax band.)

If the claim for set-off of losses within the same accounting period has, however, been made, the company may additionally claim to carry back any surplus loss against its total profits and capital gains in the 12 months preceding the accounting period that gave rise to the loss. Losses that still remain unrelieved will be carried forward and will automatically be set off against future profits from the same trade.

Chapter 5

Corporation Tax on Capital Gains

5.1 Introduction

As explained in Chapter Three, some property companies' property disposals will give rise to trading profits rather than capital gains.

However, where a company's property disposal does fall under the capital gains regime, the calculation of the amount of capital gain chargeable to Corporation Tax (known as the 'chargeable gain') is calculated as follows:

Capital Gain = **Proceeds** Less **Base Cost**

5.2 How to Calculate the 'Proceeds'

In most cases, the amount of 'Proceeds' to be used in the calculation of a capital gain will be the actual sum received on the disposal of the asset. However, from this, the company may deduct incidental costs in order to arrive at 'net proceeds', which is the relevant sum for the purposes of calculating the capital gain.

Example
In July 2004, George Limited sells a house for £375,000. In order to make this sale, the company spent £1,500 advertising the property, paid £3,750 in estate agent's fees and paid £800 in legal fees. George Limited's net proceeds are therefore £368,950 (£375,000 less £1,500, £3,750 and £800).

Proceeds: Exceptional Situations

There are a number of cases where the proceeds we must use in the calculation of a capital gain are not simply the actual cash sum received. Three of the most common types of such exceptions are set out below.

Exception 1 – Connected persons

Where the person selling or disposing of the asset is 'connected' with the person buying or acquiring it, the open market value of the asset at the time of sale must be used in place of the actual price paid (if any).

A company will be deemed to be 'connected' with any person who controls that company, as well as close relatives of that person and other companies also controlled by that person and/or their relatives.

Example
Beckham Limited is a property investment company and is wholly owned by Victoria.

Beckham Limited sells a property to Victoria's son, Edward, for £500,000. The market value of the property at the time of this sale is £800,000. The company pays legal fees of £475 on the sale.

Beckham Limited will be deemed to have received net sale proceeds of £800,000 (the market value). The legal fees the company has borne are irrelevant, as this was not an 'arm's-length' transaction.

The concept of 'connected persons' is important for a number of reasons, as we will see later in the guide.

Exception 2 – Transactions not at 'arm's-length'

Where a transaction takes place between 'connected persons' as above, there is an automatic assumption that the transaction is not at 'arm's-length' and hence market value must always be substituted for the actual proceeds.

There are, however, other instances where the transaction may not be at 'arm's-length', such as:

- A sale of an asset to an employee
- A transaction that is part of a larger transaction
- A transaction that is part of a series of transactions

The effect of these is much the same as before – the asset's market value must be used in place of the actual proceeds, if any.

The key difference from Exception 1 above is that the onus of proof that this is not an 'arm's-length' transaction is on the Inland Revenue, rather than there being an automatic assumption that this is the case.

Example
Brooklyn Limited owns an investment property with a market value of £200,000. If the company sold the property at this price, it would have a capital gain of £80,000.

Not wishing to incur a Corporation Tax liability, Brooklyn Limited decides instead to sell the house to Romeo Limited for £120,000. However, Brooklyn Limited only does this on condition that Romeo Limited gives it an interest-free loan of £80,000 for an indefinite period.

The condition imposed by Brooklyn Limited means that this transaction is not at 'arm's-length'. The correct position is therefore that Brooklyn Limited should be deemed to have sold the property for £200,000 and still have a capital gain of £80,000.

Exception 3 – Non-cash proceeds

Sometimes all or part of the sale consideration will take a form other than cash.

The sale proceeds to be taken into account in these cases will be the market value of the assets or rights received in exchange for the asset sold.

Example
Little Property Company Limited owns an office block in central London.

Big Properties plc (a quoted company) wants to buy the property from Little Property Company Limited but, as it is experiencing some short-term cash-flow difficulties, it offers Little Property Company Limited 500,000 shares for the property rather than cash.

Little Property Company Limited accepts this offer and takes the shares, which are worth £1.25 per share at the date of sale.

Little Property Company Limited's sale proceeds for Corporation Tax purposes will therefore be £625,000 (500,000 x £1.25).

Wealth Warning

Note that if, as in the above example, you take non-cash consideration for a sale, you will be taxed on the value of that consideration at that date. If the value of the non-cash asset which you receive should subsequently fall, you will still be taxed on the original value!

This problem can sometimes possibly be alleviated by disposing of the asset which has fallen in value and thus generating a capital loss, but:

- This is not always desirable, and

- A capital loss cannot be carried back to an earlier accounting period.

5.3 How to Calculate the 'Base Cost'

The 'Base Cost' is the amount that may be deducted in the capital gains calculation in respect of an asset's cost. The higher the base cost, the lower the chargeable gain and the less Corporation Tax payable!

As with 'Proceeds', in most cases, the basic starting point will be the actual amount paid.

Added to the actual amount paid are:

- Incidental costs of acquisition (e.g. legal fees, Stamp Duty, etc).

- Enhancement expenditure (e.g. the cost of building an extension to a property).

- Expenditure incurred in establishing, preserving or defending title to, or rights over, the asset (e.g. legal fees incurred as a result of a boundary dispute).

Base Cost – Special Situations

As before with 'Proceeds', there are a number of special situations where base cost is determined by reference to something other than the actual amount paid for the asset.

The major exceptions fall into two main categories:

- The asset was acquired before 31st March 1982.

- The asset was not acquired by way of a 'bargain at arm's length'

Assets acquired before 31st March 1982

Generally speaking, the base cost will be the greater of the asset's actual cost or its open market value at 31st March 1982.

Where, however, the asset is sold at a loss, its base cost will be the lower of its actual cost or open market value at 31st March 1982. (This is not very likely in the context of property companies!)

Where using actual cost as the base cost produces a capital gain, but using market value at 31st March 1982 produces a capital loss, or vice versa, the asset is deemed to have been sold at neither a gain nor a loss.

Assets Not Acquired by Way of a 'Bargain At Arm's Length'

In the case of an acquisition that is not a 'bargain at arm's length', the acquiring company's base cost will generally be the asset's market value at the time of purchase, as this will be the deemed 'proceeds' on which the person selling the asset is taxed.

Example

Martin owns a property investment company called Johnson Limited.

Johnson Limited buys a warehouse from Martin for £100,000. The warehouse, however, has an open market value of £200,000.

Johnson Limited will therefore have a Base Cost for the warehouse of £200,000.

(Note, however, that Martin's personal Capital Gains Tax liability will be based on a sale for deemed 'proceeds' of £200,000.)

Assets acquired for non-cash consideration

Where an asset was acquired for non-cash consideration, its base cost will be determined by reference to the market value of the consideration given.

5.4 How to Calculate Indexation Relief

Indexation relief was introduced in 1982 to eliminate the purely inflationary element of capital gains.

Unlike individuals, for whom indexation relief was 'frozen' in April 1998, companies continue to accumulate indexation relief on their capital assets.

The relief is based on the increase in the retail prices index over the period of the asset's ownership (or from 31st March 1982 until the date of sale, if the asset was acquired before then).

Where the base cost of the asset is made up of original cost and later enhancement expenditure, each element of the base cost will attract indexation relief at its own appropriate rate.

Example

Wilkinson Limited bought a property for £100,000 in June 1987.

In August 1991, the company spent £50,000 building an extension to the property. The property was sold for £600,000 in November 2004.

The Retail Prices Index was 101.9 in June 1987, 134.1 in August 1991 and 186.4 in November 2004 (I made the last one up, because it hasn't been published yet.)

The Retail Prices Index increased by 82.9% between June 1987 and November 2004 so the indexation relief due on the company's original purchase cost is £82,900 (£100,000 x 82.9%).

The Retail Prices Index increased by 39.0% between August 1991 and November 2004, so the indexation relief due on the company's enhancement expenditure (i.e. the cost of the extension) is £19,500 (£50,000 x 39.0%).

Wilkinson Limited's chargeable gain is therefore calculated as follows:

	£	£
Sale proceeds		*600,000*
Less:		
Original cost	*100,000*	
Enhancement expenditure	*50,000*	
		(150,000)
Indexation relief		
On original cost	*82,900*	
On enhancement expenditure	*19,500*	
Total:		*(102,400)*
Chargeable gain on which		
Corporation Tax will be payable:		*£347,600*

It should be noted that indexation relief may not be used to create or increase a capital loss. Hence, in some cases, the amount of relief has to be restricted. Where a capital loss already arises, no relief is given at all. Where there is a capital gain before indexation, the relief must be restricted to the amount of the gain before indexation.

Example
Wilkinson Limited has a second property. The original purchase date and cost of this second property is exactly the same as in the previous example and the company also incurred enhancement expenditure of exactly the same amount and at exactly the same time as in the first example.

However, the second property has a structural fault and Wilkinson Limited is only able to sell it for £200,000 in November 2004.

The company's chargeable gain on the disposal of this second property is calculated as follows:

	£	£
Sale proceeds		200,000
Less:		
Original cost	100,000	
Enhancement expenditure	50,000	
		(150,000)
Indexation relief		
On original cost	82,900	
On enhancement expenditure	19,500	
Total:	(102,400)	
But restricted to:		(50,000)
Chargeable gain on which Corporation Tax will be payable:		NIL

5.5 Making the Most of Capital Losses

Any capital losses that arise may be set off against chargeable gains (after indexation relief) of the same accounting period.

Surplus capital losses are then carried forward and set off against chargeable gains of later accounting periods.

Tax Tip

Unless there are strong commercial reasons for doing so, a company which has unused capital losses carried forward should not be wound up as there will always be a possibility of realising tax-free capital gains through it in the future.

Chapter 6

The Importance of Taper Relief

6.1 Shares Held Since 6th April 2000

In Chapter Three, we briefly considered the position of the shareholder on a sale of the company's shares.

As already discussed, the shareholder's potential Capital Gains Tax liability is dependent on whether the shares in the company are considered to be 'business assets' for taper relief purposes.

Generally speaking, as already discussed in section 3.6, for a company's shares to be regarded as 'business assets' for taper relief purposes, the company must not be carrying on any 'substantial' non-trading activities.

If a company meets this requirement then it is referred to as a 'trading company' for taper relief purposes.

Since 6th April 2000, an individual's shares in a company have qualified as 'business assets' for taper relief purposes under any of the following circumstances:

i)   Whenever the company is an unquoted trading company. (Broadly, this means that, in addition to qualifying as a trading company, the company must also not be listed on any recognised stock exchange.)

ii) When the company is a quoted trading company and the individual is an officer or employee of that company or of another company that is a member of the same group of companies or which may reasonably be considered to be part of the same commercial association of companies.

iii) When the company is a quoted trading company and the individual owns enough shares to enable at least 5% of the voting rights in the company to be exercised.

iv) When the individual is an officer or employee of the company, or of another company as in (ii) above, and does not have a 'material interest' in the company.

     Broadly speaking, this means that the individual concerned, together with any 'connected persons' (see Appendix B) does not hold, and cannot control, more than 10% of any class of shares in the company.

Summary So Far

In practice, what all of this means for the vast majority of small property companies is that the shares will only be 'business assets' for taper relief purposes if the company itself is a trading company.

6.2 Shares Held Before 6th April 2000

Before 6th April 2000, the rules were even more restrictive. Before then, shares could only be 'business assets' if:

i)   The company was a trading company, and

ii)   Either

    a. The individual shareholder held at least 25% of the voting rights in the company, or

    b. The shareholder was a full-time working officer of the company **and** held at least 5% of the voting rights in the company.

This more restrictive earlier definition is still important to shareholders who have held shares since before 6th April 2000. If their shares only qualify as 'business assets' under the new definition, they will not get the full rate of 'business asset' taper relief (see below) unless they hold on to those shares until at least 6th April 2010.

Any sales of such shares in the meantime will attract a 'hybrid' rate of taper relief which is a mixture of the 'business asset' rate and the 'non-business asset' rate. The 'hybrid' rate applying will gradually increase as we approach 6th April 2010. See section 6.5 below for more details on the potential impact of this 'hybrid' rate of taper relief, as well as regarding a possible method to overcome its effect.

6.3 So What's the Big Deal About Taper Relief?

Oh, it's a big deal all right!

For disposals of shares that qualified as 'business assets' for the whole of the individual's ownership (or since 6th April 1998, if held before then) taking place on or after 6th April 2002, the rate of taper relief applying is:

- 50% for shares held for at least one year, but less than two, prior to sale.

- 75% for shares held for two years or more prior to sale.

This means a maximum effective Capital Gains Tax rate on sales of such shares after two years of only 10% (40% tax on just 25% of the capital gain).

Shares that do not qualify as 'business assets', however, are only eligible for taper relief as follows:

- For shares held less than three years: Nil

- For shares held for three years but less than four: 5%

- For shares held for four years but less than five: 10%

- For shares held for five years but less than six: 15%

- For shares held for six years but less than seven: 20%

- For shares held for seven years but less than eight: 25%

- For shares held for eight years but less than nine: 30%

- For shares held for nine years but less than ten: 35%

- For shares held for ten years or more: 40%

To illustrate the importance of taper relief further, let's look at an example.

Example

Redpath Limited and Delaglio Limited are both property development companies.

Both companies were set up for an initial investment of only £1,000 each on 1st January 2003, when they also both started trading.

Both companies also have some rental income, meaning that, in the Inland Revenue's view they have some non-trading activity.

Redpath Limited, however, manages to keep the non-trading activity below the level that the Inland Revenue regard as substantial (see section 3.6), meaning that it is accepted as a trading company. The shares in Redpath Limited are therefore 'business assets' for taper relief purposes.

Brian, who owns all of the shares in Redpath Limited, decides to wind the company up in 2005 and receives net proceeds from this of £1,001,000.

Brian's gain of £1,000,000 is reduced by taper relief at 75% to a tapered gain of £250,000. Assuming he is a higher rate taxpayer and has used up his annual exemption on other gains, his Capital Gains Tax liability on the sale of his Redpath Limited shares will be £100,000.

Delaglio Limited's non-trading activities have unfortunately exceeded the level that the Inland Revenue regard as substantial, meaning that the company is not regarded as a trading company for taper relief purposes.

Lawrence, the sole shareholder of Delaglio Limited, also winds his company up in 2005 and also makes a capital gain of £1,000,000.

Lawrence's shares in Delaglio Limited are 'non-business assets' for taper relief purposes and, as he has held them for less than three years, he is not entitled to any taper relief at all!

Hence, assuming that Lawrence is also a higher rate taxpayer and has used up his annual exemption on other gains, his Capital Gains Tax liability on the sale of his Delaglio Limited shares will be £400,000.

That's £300,000 more, or FOUR TIMES AS MUCH as Brian's Capital Gains Tax liability on a sale of very similar shares.

As I said, taper relief is indeed a 'Big Deal'!

6.4 Shares Held Before 6th April 1998

The taper relief rates for non-business assets, as set out above, have to be adapted in the case of shares that were already held when taper relief was first introduced on 6th April 1998. Two adjustments are required:

- Firstly, in applying the ownership periods set out above, any period of ownership prior to 6th April 1998 is disregarded, but

- To compensate for this, an additional year is counted in respect of any shares held before 17th March 1998.

Example

Kenny has held his shares in Logan Limited, a property investment company (i.e. not a trading company), since 11th February 1998. He sells his shares on 15th April 2004.

*For taper relief purposes, Kenny will be regarded as having held his shares for six years (the number of whole years between 6th April 1998 and 15th April 2004) **plus** one additional year (for having held the shares on 17th March 1998), i.e. seven years in total.*

Kenny is therefore entitled to taper relief of 25%.

Tax Tip

For shares held since before the introduction of the taper relief regime on 6th April 1998, the beginning of each tax year, up to and including 6th April 2007, will herald an increase in the amount of taper relief available.

Hence, in such cases, it may very often be worth delaying a sale of shares until the new tax year, if there are no other factors weighing against this.

6.5 What If Shares Were Only Sometimes 'Business Assets'?

Where shares only qualified as 'business assets' for part of the individual's period of ownership (or for part of the period since 6th April 1998, if the shares were held before then), the 'hybrid' rate of taper relief will again apply and the full 'business asset' rate will only be available when 10 years have expired since the last date on which the shares did not qualify as 'business assets'.

Shares which are subject to this 'hybrid' rate are also sometimes referred to as having 'tainted taper'.

Example

Thompson Limited is a property development company and is regarded as a trading company for taper relief purposes.

Steve has held 4% of the company's shares since 1995.

On 6th April 2004, Steve sells his shares in Thompson Limited and realises a capital gain of £1,200,000 after indexation relief.

Steve's shares will be regarded as having qualified as a 'business asset' since 6th April 2000. This represents four years out of his six years of ownership within the taper relief regime (i.e. since 6th April 1998).

Hence, four sixths of Steve's gain is eligible for business asset taper relief. The remaining two sixths is only eligible for non-business asset taper relief.

Steve's taper relief therefore works out as follows:

> Business asset taper relief
> £1,200,000 x 4/6 x 75% =   £600,000
>
> Non-business asset taper relief
> £1,200,000 x 2/6 x 25%* =   £100,000
>
> Total   £700,000

Steve thus gets an overall effective rate of taper relief of 58.3%, part way between the more beneficial business asset rate and the slower non-business asset rate.

* - Steve qualifies for the 'bonus year' here, thus giving him an effective seven years' ownership for non-business asset taper relief purposes, as explained in section 6.3.

Timing

Where tainted taper applies, the timing of sales will make a difference to the eventual outcome. To illustrate this, let's return to our example.

Example Part 2
Steve decides to delay the sale of his shares until 6th April 2005. As before, Steve's shares will be regarded as having qualified as a 'business asset' since 6th April 2000. This now represents five years out of seven years of ownership within the taper relief regime.

Hence, five sevenths of Steve's gain will now be eligible for business asset taper relief, with the remaining two sevenths continuing to be eligible for non-business asset taper relief.

Steve's taper relief therefore now works out as follows:

Business asset taper relief £1,200,000 x 5/7 x 75% =	£642,857
Non-business asset taper relief £1,200,000 x 2/7 x 30% =	£102,857
Total	£745,714

The delay in Steve's share sale has thus increased his overall effective rate of taper relief by 3.8% to 62.1%. This will have saved him £18,286 in Capital Gains Tax.

Steve's Capital Gains Tax saving arises for two reasons:

i)   The proportion of his gain qualifying for business asset taper relief has increased (from 66.7% to 71.4%). Although, in this example, we have been working in whole years for simplicity, this increase actually takes place gradually, on a day-by-day basis.

ii)   The rate of taper relief on the non-business portion of the gain has increased. This increase only takes place in annual increments (see sections 6.3 and 6.4 above).

Is it Worth Waiting?

In Steve's case, one would really have to say "probably not". A year's delay has only increased his after-tax sale proceeds by around 1.8%. This is not much of a rate of return and small compensation for the commercial risk involved.

However, one doesn't always have to actually wait:

Tax Tip

A sale of shares to another company which qualifies for business asset taper relief purposes (see section 6.1), in exchange for shares in <u>that</u> company, would enable the shareholder to hold over his or her capital gain until they sell those new shares.

By the time of the later sale, the shareholder's taper relief entitlement will have increased.

Wealth Warning

In applying the above strategy, it is essential that the new company is a qualifying company for business asset taper relief purposes. If the new company does not qualify, the strategy will backfire and the amount of taper relief available will actually reduce!

Combating Tainted Taper

Tainted taper lasts for up to ten years. It will therefore often be worth considering taking steps to combat it.

A transfer of shares with tainted taper into a trust will re-start the taper relief clock and will often allow maximum taper relief to be obtained in two years instead of ten.

Unfortunately, however, from 10th December 2003, any transfers of shares into a "self-interested trust" may potentially give rise to an immediate Capital Gains Tax liability. This applies whenever the transferor or their spouse is able to benefit from the transferee trust.

Tainted Taper is, of course, a direct result of Gordon Brown's inability to leave the taper relief regime alone and his resultant constant tinkering with it. It is therefore rather objectionable that the same person who has caused these problems has also seen fit to block the main method available for alleviating them.

Nevertheless, transfers of shares with tainted taper into a trust are still worth considering under the following circumstances:

- Where the transferee trust has different beneficiaries (e.g. children of the transferor).

- Where a disposal of the shares would not currently give rise to any significant Capital Gains Tax liability.

- Where the Capital Gains Tax liability arising now is far outweighed by the likely future savings (although this does, of course, carry a major element of risk).

6.6 Shares Transferred Between Husband and Wife

Where shares are transferred between husband and wife prior to sale, the taper relief available on the ultimate disposal will be calculated by reference to the total period of ownership of both spouses.

However, in deciding whether the shares qualify as 'business assets' for all or part of this combined period of ownership, reference will be made only to the ownership history of the spouse making the final disposal.

Wealth Warning

Transfers of shares between husband and wife prior to sale can be highly detrimental to the rate of taper relief available.

Tax Tip

Transfers of shares between husband and wife prior to sale can be highly beneficial to the rate of taper relief available.

I suggest that you make sure that you know which one of the above applies before you make any transfers to your husband or wife.

In essence, the aim of the exercise is to ensure that the spouse making the ultimate disposal is the one with the better taper relief history for the shares, especially in the period from 6th April 1998 to 5th April 2000, when the more restrictive regime applied (see section 6.2 above).

Chapter 7

Stamp Duty & VAT For Property Companies

7.1 Introduction

Stamp Duty is the oldest tax on the statute books. It was several centuries old already when Pitt the Younger introduced Income Tax in 1799. Even today, we are still governed (to a limited extent) by the Stamp Act 1891.

From 1st December 2003, however, for transfers of real property (i.e. land and buildings or any form of legal interest in them), Stamp Duty has been replaced by Stamp Duty Land Tax (see section 7.4).

7.2 Stamp Duty on Shares

Despite talk of its abolition a few years ago (does anyone remember TAURUS?), this ancient tax does, however, continue to apply to transfers of shares.

The rate of Stamp Duty on purchases of shares and securities is still unchanged at a single uniform rate of only 0.5%. This has led to many tax-avoidance strategies, designed to avoid the excessive rates applied to property transactions by making use of this more palatable rate. However, new legislation introduced by both the 2002 and 2003 Budgets has effectively blocked most of the more popular methods.

Nevertheless, for those investing in property through a company, there remains the possibility of selling shares in that company at a much lower rate of Duty than would apply to the sale of individual properties within the company.

Wealth Warning

There are no de minimis limits for Stamp Duty and the amount payable must always be rounded up to the nearest £5.

Hence, if you decide that it's a nice idea to sell your son a share for £1, it will cost him £5 in Stamp Duty.

7.3 Goodwill

Since April 2002, companies have been exempt from Stamp Duty on purchases of goodwill.

7.4 Stamp Duty Land Tax

On 1st December 2003, the new 'Stamp Duty Land Tax' came into force for transfers of real property (i.e. land and buildings or any form of legal interest in them).

The rates of Stamp Duty Land Tax applying to transfers of property are the same for companies as they are for individuals or other property purchasers. Likewise, the type of property company that you have has no impact on the rate of Stamp Duty Land Tax.

Unfortunately, the introduction of the new tax has mainly preserved the dramatic increases in the rates of Stamp Duty that we have seen over the last few years. Stamp Duty has been at the forefront of Gordon Brown's strategy of 'stealth taxation', through which he has raised additional taxes in ways which largely go unnoticed in the media frenzy that surrounds the annual Budget process. The change to the Stamp Duty Land Tax regime has done nothing to alter this and, for larger transactions, the tax still represents a significant barrier to property investment.

The rates of Stamp Duty Land Tax (other than in 'disadvantaged areas' – see below) are as follows:

- Residential property up to £60,000 – Zero.

- Non-residential property up to £150,000 – Zero.

- Residential property over £60,000 but not more than £250,000 – 1%.

- Non-residential property over £150,000 but not more than £250,000 – 1%.

- All property over £250,000 but not more than £500,000 – 3%.

- All property over £500,000 – 4%.

All of the amounts indicated above refer to the consideration paid for the purchase – whether in cash or by any other means.

Like Stamp Duty, the Stamp Duty Land Tax payable is always rounded up to the nearest £5.

Whenever any rate less than the maximum 4% is to be applied, the purchaser is required to certify that the lower rate is properly applicable. A new, complex, and very lengthy form has been introduced for this purpose!

Furthermore, it should also be noted that the rate of Stamp Duty Land Tax to be applied must be determined after taking account of any 'associated transactions' taking place.

It can readily be seen from the above table that a small alteration in the purchase price of a property can sometimes make an enormous difference to the amount of Stamp Duty Land Tax payable.

Example

McGeehan Limited is just about to make an offer of £250,001 for a house in Edinburgh when Ian, the company's managing director, realises that the Stamp Duty Land Tax payable on this purchase, at 3%, would be £7,505. Horrified at this prospect, he amends the offer to £249,999, thus reducing the potential Stamp Duty Land Tax payable to £2,500 (1%).

This sort of change is, of course, perfectly acceptable, because the whole situation is taking place at 'arm's-length'.

However, where connected parties are involved, the Inland Revenue's Stamp Office is likely to scrutinise very closely any transactions where the consideration is only just under one of the limits set out above.

Leases

Stamp Duty Land Tax is also payable on leases (sometimes known as 'Lease Duty') and this represents one of the most significant changes from the old Stamp Duty regime. (Although Stamp Duty was often payable on leases under the old regime, it had some rather odd quirks and was open to a good deal of abuse.)

The Stamp Duty Land Tax payable on the granting of a lease is based on the 'Net Present Value' of all of the rent payable under the lease over its entire term. Where the net present value does not exceed £60,000 (for residential property) or £150,000 (for non-residential property), no Stamp Duty Land Tax will be payable. For new leases with a net present value exceeding these limits, Stamp Duty Land Tax is payable at a rate of 1% on the excess.

VAT is excluded from the rent payable under the lease for the purposes of Stamp Duty Land Tax calculations <u>unless</u> the landlord has already exercised the option to tax (this applies to commercial property only). (Previously, under the Stamp Duty regime, there was an assumption that VAT should be included in such calculations for commercial property leases, unless the lease specifically prohibited the charging of VAT.)

Example

Woodward Limited is about to take on a 10-year lease over a house in Kent at an annual rent of £12,000.

The 'Net Present Value' of the first year's rent is simply £12,000.

The second year's rent, however, has a lower 'Net Present Value' because it is not payable for 12 months. The Stamp Duty Land Tax legislation provides that the net present value of a sum of money due in 12 months' time is equal to the sum due divided by a 'discount factor'. The applicable discount factor is currently 103.5%.

Hence, the 'Present Value' of a sum of £12,000 due in 12 months' time is only £11,594 (i.e. £12,000 divided by 103.5%).

Similarly, the third year's rent, which is due a further twelve months later, must be 'discounted' again by the same amount, i.e. £11,594/103.5% = £11,202.

This process is continued for the entire 10-year life of the lease and the net present values of all of the rental payments are than added together to give the total net present value for the whole lease. In this case, this works out at £103,292.

The Stamp Duty Land Tax payable by Woodward Limited is therefore £435 (1% of £103,292 LESS £60,000, rounded up to the nearest £5).

Note that it does not matter for the purposes of this calculation whether the rent is payable monthly, quarterly or annually, or whether it is payable in advance or in arrears. Net present value is, in each case, always calculated by reference to the total annual rental payable for each year of the lease.

The current 'discount factor' (103.5%) may be changed in the future, depending on a number of factors, including the prevailing rates of inflation and interest.

Lease Premiums

Lease **premiums** also attract Stamp Duty Land Tax at the same rates as given above for outright purchases. (Special rules apply where there is also annual gross rent payable in excess of £600.)

Disadvantaged Areas

There are 2,000 areas in the UK that have been specifically designated as 'Disadvantaged Areas'. This is done by reference to postcodes in England and Wales and by reference to Electoral Wards in Scotland. (My apologies to readers with properties in Northern Ireland – I don't know how it is done there.)

These areas are sometimes also known as 'Enterprise Neighbourhoods' or 'Enterprise Areas' and, in fact, very often are not really all that 'disadvantaged' at all – so don't be fooled by the name.

A number of tax reliefs have been introduced to assist development in these areas, including some significant relaxations in the amount of Stamp Duty Land Tax payable on properties in these areas.

Residential properties within these areas are subject to the zero rate of Stamp Duty Land Tax on purchases where the consideration does not exceed £150,000.

Non-residential properties within these areas are fully exempt from Stamp Duty Land Tax.

Application to all UK Property

Stamp Duty Land Tax is payable on all transfers of UK property in accordance with the above rules regardless of where the vendor or purchaser are resident and regardless of where the transfer documentation is drawn up.

7.5 VAT

VAT, or 'Value Added Tax', to give it its proper name, is the 'new kid on the block' in UK taxation terms, having arrived on our shores from Europe on 1st January 1973.

Despite its youth, VAT is, quite probably, the UK's most hated tax and there are some nasty pitfalls awaiting the unwary property investor at the hands of this indirect form of taxation.

Unlike all of the other taxes mentioned so far in this guide, VAT is administered and collected by Her Majesty's Customs & Excise, rather than the Inland Revenue.

Residential Property Letting

Generally speaking, a property investment company, engaged primarily in residential property letting does not need to register for VAT. (Nor, indeed, very often would it be able to.)

The letting of residential property is an exempt supply for VAT purposes. VAT is therefore not chargeable on rent, although, of course, VAT cannot be recovered on expenses and the company should therefore claim VAT-inclusive costs for Corporation Tax purposes.

Beware, however, that the provision of ancillary services (e.g. cleaning or gardening) may sometimes be Standard-Rated, and hence subject to VAT at 17.5%, if the value of annual supplies of these services exceeds the registration threshold, (£58,000 from 1st April 2004). Some companies making ancillary supplies of this nature prefer to register for VAT, even if they have not reached the registration threshold, as this means that they are able to recover some of the VAT on their expenses.

Commercial Property Letting

For commercial property, there is an 'option to tax'. In other words, the landlord company may choose, for each property (on a property-by-property basis), whether or not the rent should be an exempt supply for VAT purposes.

If the 'option to tax' is exercised, the rent on the property becomes Standard Rated (at 17.5%) for VAT purposes. The landlord company may then recover VAT on all of the expenses relating to that property.

Ancillary services are again likely to be Standard Rated if supplies exceed the registration threshold.

Tax Tip

If the potential tenants of a commercial property are all, or mostly, likely to be VAT-registered businesses themselves, it will generally make sense to exercise the 'option to tax' on the property in order to recover the VAT on expenses incurred.

Property Sales

Sales of newly constructed residential property are zero-rated for VAT purposes. This means that the developer can recover all of the VAT on their construction costs without having to charge VAT on the sale of the property. (In theory, VAT is charged, but at a rate of zero.)

This treatment is extended to the sale of a property which has just been converted from a non-residential property into a residential property (*e.g. converting a barn into a house*).

It is also extended to 'substantially reconstructed protected buildings'. I will leave Customs & Excise to explain what that means!

Other sales of residential property are generally an exempt supply meaning, once again, that the company making the sale is unable to recover any of the VAT on its expenses.

Where the 'option to tax' has previously been exercised on a commercial property, the sale of that property will again be Standard Rated and this has major implications for such transactions.

Sales of new or uncompleted commercial property are Standard Rated for VAT purposes.

Property Management

Property management services are Standard Rated for VAT and hence a property management company will need to register for VAT if its annual supplies (i.e. sales) exceed the £58,000 registration threshold. It may still register voluntarily even if the level of its sales is below the threshold.

Whether the properties under the company's management are residential or commercial makes no difference for this purpose.

Naturally, a property management company that is registered for VAT can recover the VAT on most of its business expenses. There are, however, a few exceptions where VAT cannot be wholly recovered (*e.g. on the purchase of motor cars*).

Interaction with Corporation Tax

Any company that is registered for VAT should generally include only the net (i.e. excluding VAT) amounts of income and expenditure in its accounts. Where VAT recovery is barred or restricted (*e.g. on the provision of private fuel for directors or staff*), however, the additional cost arising may generally be claimed as an expense for Corporation Tax purposes.

A non-registered business should include the VAT in its business expenditure for Corporation Tax purposes.

Chapter 8

Saving Tax When You Extract Profits

8.1 Introduction

As I explained at the beginning of the guide, the need to extract profits from your property company (or any company) poses a major drawback. This is why property companies generally work better if the owners do not continually draw out all or most of the profits.

Clearly, if you are able to retain all of the profits within the company, profit extraction is not a problem.

However, sooner or later, almost everyone will want to take something out of the company, or else there wouldn't be much point in having a property business in the first place!

8.2 Profit Extraction Methods

There are two main methods for extracting profits from your own company:

i)   Paying yourself a salary or a bonus (i.e. employment income), or

ii)   Paying yourself dividends.

Salaries, Etc

Employment income is subject to Income Tax and to both employer's and employee's National Insurance Contributions.

Payments of wages, salaries or bonuses are deductible against the company's taxable profits for Corporation Tax purposes, as long as they are incurred for the benefit of the company's business. Some care needs to be taken, therefore, if you do decide to pay yourself, your spouse, or any other members of your family, any wages or salaries, as no deduction will be available if there is no business justification for the payment.

In other words, yes, the recipient does have to actually work in the business!

Tax Tip

Subject to my comments above, payment of a salary equal to the personal allowance (£4,745 for the 2004/2005 tax year) to yourself, your spouse or another adult family member can be a useful tax-planning measure, where justified.

Dividends

Dividends are subject to Income Tax at rates of 32.5% for higher rate taxpayers and 10% for all other taxpayers. However, before being taxed, dividends from UK companies must be grossed up for a non-refundable tax credit equal to one-ninth of the dividend paid. This tax credit may then be set off against the Income Tax arising.

The net result of this rather complex system is that higher rate taxpayers pay an effective rate of 25% on dividends received from UK companies and all other taxpayers have no further tax to pay on UK dividends received.

Dividends represent a distribution of a company's after-tax profits and no deduction is therefore allowed for Corporation Tax purposes. Furthermore, from 1st April 2004, the payment of a dividend can result in an increase in the amount of Corporation Tax payable by smaller companies (see section 2.3).

No business justification is required for dividends, although company law does require distributable profits to be available.

Hence, subject to the comments that follow, having your spouse or another adult family member as a shareholder in your company may be a useful tax-planning measure. (Note that dividends paid to minor children from their parent's own company will be treated as the parent's own income for tax purposes.)

Wealth Warning 1

The Inland Revenue have recently been attacking some arrangements involving complex share structures that effectively enable the husband or wife of the main controlling shareholder to receive dividend income without their having any real involvement in the company or its business.

Keeping the share structure to a single class of ordinary shares should avoid these problems.

Wealth Warning 2

Where shares are held jointly by husband and wife, it is no longer possible for the dividend income arising to be automatically split 50/50 for Income Tax purposes. The income must now be split according to the couple's actual beneficial entitlement to it.

The relative merits of salaries and bonuses or dividends depends on the company's profit levels, as well as the recipient's own tax position. This complex issue is examined in detail in the Taxcafe.co.uk guide *Bonus versus Dividends*.

Chapter 9

Personal vs Company Ownership

9.1 Introduction

In the previous chapters, we have worked through the principles of how a property company and its owners are taxed.

In the next chapter, we will be looking in detail at the decision itself – i.e. "Should I run my property business through a company?"

Before we do that, however, we are going to take a quick look in this chapter at the comparative level of tax on a personal property investor or a company investing in property.

There are a great many different criteria that we could choose for our comparison. Almost an infinite number, in fact.

However, in order to keep things down to a manageable size, we are just going to look at a few different scenarios which, I believe, should be sufficient to amply demonstrate the principles involved.

In this chapter we will mostly be looking only at income. Once we get into capital gains, the situation becomes even more complicated and can only really be assessed through the use of detailed examples. This will form a major part of the next chapter.

It is important to remember, as you consider the tables shown in this chapter, that these only represent one-off annual 'snapshots' of the position. While they do provide useful illustrations of the potential tax savings involved, I must urge you to also consider the more detailed and longer-term issues which we will be looking at in the next chapter.

All of the tax calculations given in this chapter are based on 2004/2005 tax rates for individuals (see Appendix C) and on the latest Corporation Tax rates, as explained in Chapter Two.

9.2 Rental Profits Kept in the Company

The tax burden on an individual or a company receiving rental income only (and having no other taxable income or gains) may be compared as follows:

Annual Rental Profits	Tax Paid Personally	Tax Paid By Company	Tax Saving
£5,000	£26	£0	£26
£10,000	£914	£0	£914
£15,000	£2,014	£1,188	£826
£20,000	£3,114	£2,375	£739
£25,000	£4,214	£3,563	£651
£30,000	£5,314	£4,750	£564
£40,000	£8,208	£7,125	£1,083
£50,000	£12,208	£9,500	£2,708
£75,000	£22,208	£14,250	£7,958
£100,000	£32,208	£19,000	£13,208
£150,000	£52,208	£28,500	£23,708
£200,000	£72,208	£38,000	£34,208

Assumptions

In this scenario, it is assumed that:

i)   The company does not have any associated companies (see section 14.4).

ii)   The company's accounting period is 12 months.

iii)   The individual is not entitled to any additional allowances, other than the normal personal allowance (£4,745).

iv)   Company profits are retained.

9.3 Rental Profits Extracted from the Company

Here we are looking at exactly the same scenario as in section 9.2 (i.e. rental profits only and no other income), but with the difference that all of the company's after-tax profits are paid out to the individual shareholder as dividends. All other assumptions remain the same.

The 'Tax paid via company' column here summarises the total tax burden using the company route, including both the Corporation Tax payable by the company and the individual's Income Tax on the dividends received. It can readily be seen that the tax savings are, at best, vastly reduced, whilst, at lower profit levels, there is now an overall tax cost to using the company.

Annual Rental Profits	Tax Paid Personally	Tax Paid By Company	Tax Saving or Cost
£5,000	£26	£798	-£773
£10,000	£914	£1,597	-£683
£15,000	£2,014	£2,566	-£552
£20,000	£3,114	£3,547	-£434
£25,000	£4,214	£4,535	-£321
£30,000	£5,314	£5,525	-£211
£40,000	£8,208	£7,511	£697
£50,000	£12,208	£11,492	£715
£75,000	£22,208	£21,305	£903
£100,000	£32,20	£31,117	£1,090
£150,000	£52,208	£50,742	£1,465
£200,000	£72,208	£70,367	£1,840

These results lead us to the general conclusion that a property company is of little or no benefit if all of its profits are being extracted by the owner each year.

9.4 The 'Optimum Scenario'

This scenario is the middle ground between the two previous sections.

Here I am assuming that the shareholder takes a salary equal to his or her personal allowance (£4,745), plus dividends of £28,260 (except where the company has insufficient profits available for this level of dividend, when the maximum available will be taken).

This amount of dividend and salary will ensure that the individual remains beneath the higher rate Income Tax threshold. The recipient shareholder would theoretically (but see the warning below) have no Income Tax or National Insurance to pay while having a total annual income of up to £33,005.

As before, all other assumptions remain the same.

Annual Rental Profits	Tax Paid Personally	Tax Paid via Company	Tax Saving Or Cost
£5,000	£26	£41	-£15
£10,000	£914	£839	£75
£15,000	£2,014	£1,646	£368
£20,000	£3,114	£2,615	£498
£25,000	£4,214	£3,598	£616
£30,000	£5,314	£4,585	£729
£40,000	£8,208	£6,559	£1,648
£50,000	£12,208	£8,514	£3,694
£75,000	£22,208	£13,348	£8,859
£100,000	£32,208	£18,098	£14,109
£150,000	£52,208	£27,598	£24,609
£200,000	£72,208	£37,098	£35,109

As we can see, this approach has restored the benefit of the property company in all cases except where the annual profit is quite small (and even in these cases, the position is quite marginal).

Wealth Warning

In practice, this 'optimum scenario' may be a little too provocative and close Inland Revenue scrutiny can be expected!

The Inland Revenue may argue that the salary was not paid for the benefit of the trade (and is thus not deductible for Corporation Tax purposes), or may look to see if the company was able to prove that it had adequate distributable profits at the time of every dividend payment.

If dividends are paid without there being adequate evidence available to show that the company had sufficient distributable profits (**after tax**) at that time, they are illegal under company law. 'Illegal' dividends may then be treated as salary, resulting in Income Tax and National Insurance Contributions.

Meeting these exacting requirements in practice may be very difficult if trying to maintain the 'optimum scenario'.

Furthermore, the introduction of an additional Corporation Tax charge on small company dividends (see section 2.3) means that the very fact that you are paying a dividend reduces the amount of distributable profit after tax available. Solving this dilemma requires some pretty complex calculations. (I've got a maths degree and even I found them difficult!)

In reality, it is usually better to be slightly less ambitious and take a lower level of dividends. It is also important to ensure that the company quite clearly has sufficient distributable profits before any dividend is paid and has the necessary supporting records to demonstrate this fact. Documentation minuting the payment of a dividend is also advisable.

A slightly higher salary, involving a small amount of Income Tax and National Insurance Contributions may also be wise in practice.

9.5 Higher Rate Taxpayers

The situation is altered a little when the individual property investor (or prospective property company owner) has other income. It would take too long to look at every possible level of 'other income' for the individual. For simplicity, therefore, we will jump straight to an individual who is already a higher rate taxpayer before receiving any rental income.

We will assume here that the individual's 'other income' will not be put through the company. Additionally, we will assume here that profits are retained within the company.

Annual Rental Profits	Tax Paid Personally	Tax Paid via Company	Tax Saving
£5,000	£2,000	£0	£2,000
£10,000	£4,000	£0	£4,000
£15,000	£6,000	£1,188	£4,813
£20,000	£8,000	£2,375	£5,625
£25,000	£10,000	£3,563	£6,438
£30,000	£12,000	£4,750	£7,250
£40,000	£16,000	£7,125	£8,875
£50,000	£20,000	£9,500	£10,500
£75,000	£30,000	£14,250	£15,750
£100,000	£40,000	£19,000	£21,000
£150,000	£60,000	£28,500	£31,500
£200,000	£80,000	£38,000	£42,000

Other Assumptions

It is, perhaps, time to repeat our other assumptions, which remain unaltered here:

i) The company does not have any associated companies (see section 14.4).
ii) The company's accounting period is 12 months.
iii) The individual is not entitled to any additional allowances, other than the normal personal allowance (£4,745).
iv) Company profits are retained.

9.6 Extracting Profits Revisited

Here we are looking at the position for a higher rate taxpayer who extracts all of the company's profits as dividends. As before, the 'Tax Paid via Company' column summarises the total tax burden using the company route, including both the Corporation Tax payable by the company and the individual's Income Tax on the dividends received.

All other assumptions remain the same and so does the warning given at the end of section 9.4.

You will see that extracting all of the profits is again highly detrimental to the tax savings.

Annual Rental Profits	Tax Paid Personally	Tax Paid Via Company	Tax Saving
£5,000	£2,000	£1,849	£151
£10,000	£4,000	£3,697	£303
£15,000	£6,000	£5,674	£326
£20,000	£8,000	£7,660	£340
£25,000	£10,000	£9,651	£349
£30,000	£12,000	£11,644	£356
£40,000	£16,000	£15,633	£367
£50,000	£20,000	£19,625	£375
£75,000	£30,000	£29,438	£563
£100,000	£40,000	£39,250	£750
£150,000	£60,000	£58,875	£1,125
£200,000	£80,000	£78,500	£1,500

9.7 Trading Profits

Having covered rental profits, it is worth taking a look at the same comparison where the income from the property business is treated as trading income.

This makes no difference to the rates of Corporation Tax applying. The individual's tax position is significantly altered however, due to the fact that National Insurance Contributions (both Class 2 and Class 4) are payable where this income is received personally.

We will assume here that the individual has no other income and that the 'optimum scenario' (see section 9.4) is followed for the distribution of profits (for illustration purposes only). All other assumptions remain the same and, as usual, I would draw your attention to the warning in section 9.4.

As usual, the 'Tax paid via company' column summarises the total tax burden using the company route. The 'Tax paid personally' column represents the total of both Income Tax and National Insurance Contributions. I have added an additional column here, 'Extra savings', which shows how much more tax the company is saving than in the rental income scenario already considered in section 9.4. As you can see, this demonstrates the fact that a company can produce even greater savings where the underlying property business is classed as a trading activity.

Trading Profits	Tax Paid Personally	Tax Paid via Company	Tax Saving	Extra Saving
5,000	155	41	114	129
10,000	1,443	839	604	529
15,000	2,943	1,646	1,297	929
20,000	4,443	2,615	1,827	1,329
25,000	5,943	3,598	2,345	1,729
30,000	7,443	4,585	2,858	2,129
40,000	10,557	6,559	3,998	2,349
50,000	14,657	8,514	6,143	2,449
75,000	24,907	13,348	11,559	2,699
100,000	35,157	18,098	17,059	2,949
150,000	55,657	27,598	28,059	3,449
200,000	76,157	37,098	39,059	3,949

9.8 Capital Gains

Finally, in this chapter, it is worth taking a quick look at the difference in the tax on a typical capital gain on a property held by an individual investor or by a property investment company.

In this scenario, we will assume the following:

- The property was purchased for £100,000 in June 1999 and sold in July 2004 producing a total gain before exemptions and reliefs equal to the amount shown in the first column below.

- The property is a 'non-business asset' for taper relief purposes.

- The indexation relief rate over the relevant period is 10.9%.

- Neither the company nor the individual investor have made any other capital gains during the same period.

- No other reliefs or exemptions are available to either the individual or the company.

- Neither the company nor the individual investor have any taxable income for the period.

- The company does not have any associated companies (see section 14.4).

- The company's accounting period is 12 months.

- Company profits are retained.

Capital Gain Before Reliefs	Tax Paid Personally	Tax Paid By Company	Tax Saving
£5,000	£0	£0	£0
£10,000	£30	£0	£30
£15,000	£708	£0	£708
£20,000	£1,558	£0	£1,558
£25,000	£2,408	£974	£1,434
£30,000	£3,258	£2,161	£1,097
£40,000	£4,958	£4,536	£422
£50,000	£7,238	£6,911	£327
£75,000	£15,738	£12,179	£3,559
£100,000	£24,238	£16,929	£7,309
£150,000	£41,238	£26,429	£14,809
£200,000	£58,238	£35,929	£22,309

Naturally, all of this is rather contrived, but it is perhaps the best that we can come up with by way of a simple illustration of the impact of the different tax regimes.

Most importantly, readers should remember that no account has been taken here of the potential additional tax costs involved in extracting the sale proceeds from the company. Far more detailed analysis of the impact of the difference between the two regimes is given in the next chapter.

Chapter 10

Making the Big Decision

10.1 The 'Big Picture'

Before you can decide whether a company is for you or not, you will need to look at what I call the 'Big Picture'.

Many investors concentrate almost exclusively on the taxation treatment of their income. Others are mainly concerned with capital gains.

Neither approach is correct. The only way to carry out effective tax planning is to take every applicable tax into account. In the case of property investment companies, we are not concerned only with income, nor solely with capital gains, but with both. On top of that, we must also consider the costs of extracting rental profits and sale proceeds from the company.

VAT, Stamp Duty, Stamp Duty Land Tax and any other tax costs should also be considered and, if one is taking the really long view, it makes sense to give some thought to Inheritance Tax as well.

Fully effective tax planning is only possible once all potential tax costs have been taken into account, however and whenever they are likely to arise.

But, even this is still not truly the 'Big Picture'.

Bayley says:

> "The truly wise investor does not seek to minimise the amount of tax paid, but rather to maximise the **wealth** remaining once all taxes have been taken into account."

10.2 Types Of Property Business Revisited

At this stage, it is already reasonable to summarise that the current tax regime produces the potential to make significant tax savings by operating most property development, property trading or property management businesses through a company.

This arises mainly because of the preferential Corporation Tax rates when compared with the combined Income Tax and National Insurance Contributions cost of trading on a personal basis.

Add to this the fact that a trading company's shares will qualify for 75% taper relief for Capital Gains Tax purposes after only two years of ownership and the position appears fairly clear-cut.

The introduction of the new Corporation Tax charge for small company dividends has merely served to slightly diminish the advantages of a small trading company. However, as we saw in section 9.7, it has certainly not eliminated them.

The only danger seems to lie in potential further changes to the tax regime or, perhaps, with the investor's inability to comply with the more stringent administrative necessities involved in operating a company.

The position for property investment companies, however, is rather less certain and hence this is where we are going to concentrate for most of the remainder of this chapter.

10.3 The Rental Income Position

In the preceding chapters, we have looked at the mechanics of how UK resident companies are taxed.

We will now begin to look at how this all affects property investment businesses and whether a company therefore becomes beneficial or not.

The best way to illustrate this is by way of an example.

Example 'A', Part 1
Humphrey has decided to begin investing in property with the intention of building up a property portfolio over the next few years. He is already a higher rate taxpayer, even before taking any rental income into consideration.

Although his friend Charlie said "you'd be daft not to use a company, old boy", in April 2004, Humphrey goes ahead and buys six flats in his own name for £100,000 each and begins to rent them out.

During the following year, Humphrey receives rental income of £10,000 from each flat, but has deductible expenditure totalling £28,000 (including mortgage interest), leaving him with a profit of £32,000. Humphrey's accountant, Edmund, therefore advises him that he has an Income Tax liability of £12,800 (£32,000 at 40%).

Feeling somewhat frustrated by his inability to persuade Humphrey to invest through a limited company, Charlie decides to try it out for himself. He sets up a company, Murrayfield Limited, and, through this, he too buys six flats for £100,000 each. He incurs the same level of expenses as Humphrey and Murrayfield Limited thus has a taxable profit of £32,000.

The first £10,000 of Murrayfield Limited's profits are tax free, with the remaining £22,000 being taxed at an effective rate of 23.75%. The Corporation Tax payable by Murrayfield Limited is thus £5,225.

At first glance, therefore, Charlie appears to be some £7,575 better off than Humphrey, indicating that a company seems to be highly beneficial.

Now feeling rather pleased with himself, Charlie shows what he has done to Edmund (who happens to be his accountant too). Unfortunately for Charlie, Edmund has three pieces of bad news for him.

Firstly, as using a company has a few extra complications, Edmund's fees to Charlie will be rather more than he charged Humphrey. However, the difference is not a huge sum compared to the tax he has saved, and is a tax-deductible expense in itself, so Charlie is not too concerned by this.

Secondly though, Edmund points out that if Charlie wants any of the money that Murrayfield Limited has made, he will have to pay himself a dividend. When he receives this dividend, Charlie, who is also a higher rate taxpayer, will have to pay Income Tax on it at an effective rate of 25%.

Thirdly, under the new small company dividend regime, Murrayfield Limited will incur an additional Corporation Tax charge when it pays any dividends to Charlie. As the company's effective average rate of Corporation Tax is 16.33%, there will be an additional charge of 2.67% on any amounts paid out to Charlie as a dividend

Hence, (ignoring Edmund's additional fees for the sake of illustration), the maximum dividend that Charlie can take out of Murrayfield Limited is £26,078. This sum is arrived at by dividing the remaining profits available after the initial Corporation Tax charge (£26,775) by 102.67% (i.e. one plus the additional Corporation Tax charge rate).

Charlie's dividend gives rise to an additional Corporation Tax charge of £697 (£26,078 at 2.67%). Charlie also has an Income Tax liability of £6,519 on his dividend (25% of £26,078).

In total, Charlie's overall tax burden therefore amounts to £12,441 (Corporation Tax of £5,225 and £697 plus Income Tax of £6,519).

Note that, for the sake of illustration, I am basing Murrayfield Limited's additional Corporation Tax charge on its effective average rate of Corporation Tax for the year in which the profits arise. In reality, the calculation will be made by reference to the company's Corporation Tax position for the year in which the dividends are paid. However, if, as in many cases, Charlie were taking his dividends out during the year, as the profits arise, the position would, in any case, be exactly as shown in the example anyway.

Analysis of Example 'A' so Far

In purely tax terms, Charlie remains £359 better off than Humphrey. After taking account of Edmund's higher fees and other costs associated with running a company, Charlie is probably not really any better off than Humphrey. This is mainly because Charlie has withdrawn all of his rental profits from the company by way of dividend.

In this example, we have examined the position of two higher rate taxpayers who both want to spend all of the profits from their property business. The example indicates that a company is of little benefit in this situation.

Humphrey and Charlie are typical of the type of property investor who already has a good level of income from other sources and wishes to supplement it through property investment.

10.4 What About Taxpayers on Lower Levels of Income?

To illustrate the position for taxpayers on lower income levels, let's take a look at two other investors, Ken and Craig.

Example 'B'

The facts are the same as for Humphrey and Charlie in Example A, except that neither Ken nor Craig has any other income. Ken buys his properties personally. Craig forms a company, Cardiff Arms Park Limited, to hold his property investments.

Ken's property income of £32,000 will give him an Income Tax liability of £5,754 (at 2004/2005 rates – see Appendix C).

We will assume that Craig has taken some good advice and is following the 'Optimum Scenario' explained in section 9.4 (not forgetting to heed the warning given in that section).

This means that, after deducting Craig's salary of £4,745, Cardiff Arms Park Limited will have a taxable profit of £27,255. The initial Corporation Tax liability on this level of profit would be £4,098 (£17,255 at 23.75%) or an average effective rate of 15.04%.

The additional Corporation Tax charge on a dividend paid by Cardiff Arms Park Limited will therefore be 3.96%. Hence, Craig is able to take a dividend of 100/103.96 times the remaining profit in the company of £23,157 (£27,255 LESS £4,098). This amounts to a dividend of £22,274. As Craig is not a higher rate taxpayer, he will have no Income Tax to pay on this dividend.

The company will have an additional Corporation Tax liability of £882 (3.96% times £22,274), bringing the total tax payable up to £4,980, some £774 less than Ken.

Again then, the corporate investor is slightly better off in tax terms, but again, not by a great deal.

Conclusion

The preceding examples allow us to conclude that:

Using a company only makes a relatively small difference when all of the profits are needed to fund the investor's current lifestyle.

10.5 Reinvesting Rental Profits

In sections 10.3 and 10.4, we saw that a property investment company was of only marginal benefit when all of its profits were being withdrawn by the proprietor. In other words, the company is of little use when the rental profits are merely being used to support the investor's own lifestyle.

However, where a property investment company can produce significant financial benefits is when the property investor does not need his rental income immediately and reinvests his profits in order to build up a substantial investment portfolio over a number of years.

To see how a company may benefit these investors, let's return to our friends Humphrey and Charlie.

Example 'A', Part 2
For the next few years, Humphrey and Charlie both accumulate a property portfolio. After 10 years, each has a total of 20

properties, which have cost a total of £2,500,000. Each of them now has total annual rental income of £300,000 and annual expenditure of £100,000, leaving rental profits of £200,000.

Humphrey will face an Income Tax bill of £80,000 (£200,000 at 40%).

The Corporation Tax payable by Murrayfield Limited, on the same level of profit, will be at the small companies' rate of 19%. This amounts to £38,000.

If Charlie is still withdrawing all of his profits after tax (£162,000) as a dividend, he will also have a further £40,500 to pay in Income Tax. His total tax burden for the year would then amount to £78,500 and he would still be only £1,500 better off than Humphrey, even before taking account of the inevitable extra costs which running a company brings.

Note that, at this level of profit, Charlie would be unaffected by the new Corporation Tax charge on small company dividends.

Let us suppose instead, however, that Humphrey and Charlie each wish to reinvest £150,000 of their rental profits in a new property.

In Humphrey's case, this makes absolutely no difference to his Income Tax bill, which remains £80,000. Similarly, this reinvestment makes no difference to Murrayfield Limited's Corporation Tax bill of £38,000.

However, what the reinvestment _does_ mean is that, since Murrayfield Limited is reinvesting £150,000 of its rental profits in a new property, Charlie will only be taking out a dividend of £12,000, giving him an Income Tax bill of only £3,000. His total tax burden for the year will therefore be reduced to only £41,000, which is £39,000 less than Humphrey's!

Analysis of Example 'A', Part 2

To begin with, the example reinforces the fact that the benefit of a company remains quite marginal, even at higher levels of profit, if all of the income continues to be withdrawn.

However, it can also be seen that using a company can save a considerable amount of tax on the investor's rental profits where these are <u>not</u> all withdrawn by way of dividend (or, indeed, by any other means).

Hence, a property company proves highly beneficial for income purposes when a substantial proportion of the profits are being reinvested.

10.6 Capital Gains

In Chapter Five, we looked at the basic mechanics of how a company is taxed on its capital gains.

Now, in order to illustrate the impact of the differences between how capital gains are taxed in a company and how individuals are taxed on capital gains, let's turn to another example.

Example 'C', Part 1
In 2004, Michelle and Louise, share a lottery win. They each decide to invest £250,000 of their proceeds in property. Michelle buys her property personally, Louise forms a company, Dawson Limited, to buy her property. Both properties are rented out to provide income. In 2014, Michelle and Louise both sell their properties for £500,000.

In the intervening years, inflation has totalled 30%. Gordon Brown (now the UK's longest serving Chancellor of the Exchequer) has increased the Capital Gains Tax annual exemption to £10,000 but, in the interests of prudence, has made no other changes to the tax system (this is the least likely of all the assumptions that I have made in this guide!).

Michelle has made a capital gain of £250,000. She is entitled to taper relief at 40%, giving her a tapered gain of £150,000. After deducting her annual exemption, her taxable gain amounts to £140,000.

Michelle's Capital Gains Tax liability will amount to somewhere between £49,518 and £56,000, depending on the level of her income in 2013/2014.

Dawson Limited also has a gain of £250,000. The only relief to be deducted is indexation relief, at 30% on cost (£250,000), i.e. £75,000. This leaves Dawson Limited with a chargeable gain of £175,000. Again, the amount of tax arising depends on the level of income, but, if there are no other investments in the company, it is likely to amount to £33,250 (at the Small Companies Rate of 19%).

Again, at first glance, we see that the corporate investor appears to be better off. In fact, even at the highest possible effective rate of Corporation Tax, the tax payable by Dawson Limited (£56,875) would not be much more than that for an individual higher rate taxpayer. However, once again, we must also consider how to extract the after-tax proceeds from the company.

If Louise removes the net proceeds of £466,750 from Dawson Limited as a dividend, she would have to pay Income Tax of between £108,080 and £116,688, again depending on the level of her income in 2013/2014.

Analysis of Example 'C', Part 1

Clearly, Louise now appears to be much worse off than Michelle, but could she have done something better than simply paying herself this enormous dividend?

The answer is yes, but we will need to look at what happens to a property company which is no longer required (section 10.7) before we can see how it works.

Another alternative for Louise might be to leave the proceeds in the company for reinvestment in new property (or some other form of investment). Again, we can see from this example that a property company works best in a reinvestment environment.

In practice, however, it is highly unlikely that a property investor like Louise would have simply taken a dividend of this magnitude out of the company.

Firstly, Louise's case is unusual as she did not have any borrowings, thus meaning that the proceeds that she wished to remove from the company were somewhat inflated.

Secondly, company law would prevent her from taking a dividend out of Dawson Limited in excess of its distributable profits. (We will cover the extraction of the original capital invested in the company in section 10.7.) For the sake of illustration, therefore, let's consider Louise's tax position if she only withdraws her after-tax profit on the property from Dawson Limited, rather than her entire proceeds.

Example 'C', Part 2
Louise takes a dividend of £216,750 out of Dawson Limited, representing her after-tax profit on the sale of the property. Her Income Tax liability on this dividend will be between £45,580 and £54,188. Combining this with the Corporation Tax already suffered in Dawson Limited (£33,250), gives a total tax cost on the property disposal of between £78,830 and £87,438.

Analysis of Example 'C', Part 2

Now that we have altered the situation so that we are only looking at the profit element of the proceeds, we can clearly see that Louise, the corporate investor, is considerably worse off than Michelle, the private investor, (by approximately £30,000, regardless of the level of the investor's income).

This clearly demonstrates that a company is not a good investment vehicle if the investor wishes to realise capital gains and extract them from the company for private use, rather than reinvest them within it.

10.7 Winding Up the Company to Reduce Tax

In section 10.6 we encountered a situation where an investor was left with funds in a company that has perhaps outlived its usefulness. In such a case, the most tax-efficient procedure is to wind the company up. Unfortunately, however, this can be a very expensive process if the company still has assets and liabilities or has recently been in active business. For the sake of illustration, however, let us return to Example 'C' and ignore the impact of these costs.

Example 'C', Part 3

Rather than pay herself a large dividend, Louise decides instead to wind Dawson Limited up. Ignoring costs, this means that Dawson Limited's net proceeds of £466,750 will be distributed to Louise on the winding up and therefore be treated in her hands as a capital disposal subject to Capital Gains Tax and not Income Tax.

Louise originally invested £250,000 in Dawson Limited in order to enable it to purchase the property. Hence, her capital gain on her shares in Dawson Limited is £216,750. After taper relief of 40%, this leaves her with a tapered gain of £130,050. Deducting her annual exemption (estimated at £10,000 for 2013/2014) leaves a taxable gain of £120,050.

Louise's Capital Gains Tax liability will therefore be between £41,538 and £48,020, once again depending on the level of her income in 2013/2014. Combining this with the Corporation Tax paid by Dawson Limited gives Louise a total tax cost on this disposal of between £74,788 and £81,270.

Analysis of Example 'C', Part 3

Firstly, it is worth noting that taper relief is given on the disposal of Louise's property company shares at the 'non-business asset' rate. As explained in section 3.2, this will generally be the case for property investment companies.

By winding up the company rather than merely paying herself a dividend, Louise has improved her position a little from Part 2 (section 10.6). In effect, changing the way that her sale proceeds are treated to a capital gain (with 40% taper relief), instead of a dividend, has reduced the effective tax rate on the majority of her profits from 25% to 24%.

It's an improvement, but not much! And it still falls around £25,000 behind the tax position of Michelle, the private investor. Hence, it appears quite conclusive that a company is not beneficial when we are looking at fairly static levels of capital growth, without any serious reinvestment activity, which are ultimately being returned into the hands of the individual investor.

10.8 What if the Company Still Holds Property When Wound Up?

Generally, this would not be a good idea.

- Firstly, the costs of the winding up would be greater.

- Secondly, the company would be treated as having made a disposal of the property at its market value and taxed accordingly.

- Thirdly, the shareholder would be taxed on the 'disposal' of the company shares, again based on the market value of the property!

Example 'C' Revisited

In Louise's case, for example, tax liabilities of around £80,000 would be incurred without there being any actual sale proceeds from which to fund them.

This demonstrates the fact that, once you have your investments in a company, it can be very difficult (or expensive) to get them out if you should want to!

10.9 Reinvestment – Enormous Long-term Tax Savings

Wait a minute! Haven't we missed something here?

In section 10.5, we looked at the benefits of incorporation where some or all of the annual rental profit was being reinvested. Then, in sections 10.6 and 10.7, we looked at the taxation position on the ultimate capital gains arising in a property business.

What we have not yet considered, however, is just how the incorporated property business's long-term capital growth might benefit from its ability to reinvest a greater share of its rental profits owing to the fact that its annual tax bill on those profits is much reduced under the Corporation Tax regime.

Reinvesting Profits Over a Number of Years

We now know that a property company can produce a significantly better outcome in the short term, year on year, when its profits are being reinvested.

In Example 'A', we assumed that the investors had built up identical portfolios over a period of time. However, in practice, it is likely that if both investors reinvest all or most of their profits, the company investor will eventually build up a larger portfolio of properties. This is because the lower Corporation Tax rates will leave the company investor with extra resources to invest in new properties.

The long-term effect of reinvestment through a property company is best illustrated by way of the example that follows (Example 'D'). In this example, we will have to make a great many assumptions, including rates of return, interest rates and the rate of growth of property values.

While the real outcome over the coming years will almost certainly be different from that which is predicted here, the example will still serve as a valid illustration because we will apply all of our assumptions equally to the company investor and the personal investor, thus revealing a difference in their two outcomes which is entirely due to their different tax environments.

The numbers will get quite messy in this example. I do apologise for this, but please bear with me, as it is worth hanging on to see the ultimate overall result that arises.

Example 'D', Part 1
Lenny and Dawn each own identical rental properties, both worth £250,000. They each earn annual rents of £18,750 and, after deducting costs of £3,750, are left with annual profits of £15,000.

Lenny's property is owned personally and because he is a higher rate taxpayer he is left with after-tax profits of £9,000.

Dawn uses a company, Saunders Limited, to invest, so her rental profits are subject to Corporation Tax. The first £10,000 is tax free and the tax bill on the remaining £5,000 is £1,187.50 (at an effective Corporation Tax rate of 23.75%). Hence, after tax, Dawn is left with £13,812.50.

Now let's say each investor is using the property business to save for retirement. This means all after-tax profits are saved and reinvested.

After three years, Lenny will have £27,000 available for reinvestment. With a 70% Buy-to-Let mortgage, this will enable him to buy a new property at a cost of £90,000. Let's say this brings in rental income of £7,200, less interest of £4,410 and other costs of £1,400, leaving him with an annual rental profit of £1,390.

Lenny's total annual rental profit for both properties is now £16,390 (£15,000 PLUS £1,390). After his higher rate Income Tax at 40%, this leaves him with after-tax profits of £9,834.

Dawn, the company investor, also buys a new property after three years, but she has £41,437.50 available (3 x £13,812.50). This enables her to buy a property for £138,125, which produces rental income of £11,050. After interest of £6,768 and other costs of £1,881, Dawn's company receives an additional annual rental profit of £2,401 from this property.

Saunders Limited's annual profits are now £17,401, giving rise to Corporation Tax of £1,758 (23.75% on £7,401), leaving profits after tax of £15,643.

Analysis of Example 'D', Part 1

Already, we can see that Dawn is moving ahead of Lenny. Her company's second property purchase is worth nearly £50,000 more and her after-tax profits are now almost £6,000 per annum greater (assuming she continues to keep them within the company).

For the sake of illustration, we have had to make a number of assumptions here, which are worth explaining:

- Rental income is assumed to be 8% of the property's value.

- Mortgage interest is at 7%.

- Other annual costs amount to a fixed element of £500 per property, plus a variable element equal to 1% of the property's value.

Now let's look at Lenny and Dawn again a few years later.

Example 'D', Part 2
After another three years, Lenny has accumulated a further £29,502 of after-tax income, which he uses to purchase another new property for £98,340 (with another 70% Buy-to-Let mortgage).

Using the same assumptions as before, Lenny's new property will provide a further £1,565 in annual rental profit, bringing his total profits to £17,955.

After higher rate tax, this now produces an annual net income of £10,773 for Lenny.

This same second three-year period provides Dawn with a further £46,929 to invest. This enables Saunders Limited to purchase a new property for £156,430. As a result, the company's total annual profits will increase to £20,186, leaving £17,767 after Corporation Tax.

Analysis of Example 'D', Part 2

Dawn continues to accumulate a better portfolio than Lenny. There is now an additional £7,000 per annum of after-tax income being generated, as well as the fact that the total value of Dawn's portfolio is now around £100,000 greater than Lenny's.

We are now going to move forward many more years, assuming that the same triennial pattern of reinvestment continues for both Lenny and Dawn for another nine years (to take us 15 years from where we started).

The result in Part 3 will be based on all of the same assumptions as in Parts 1 and 2 above, assuming, in turn, that these all remain valid throughout that period.

Additionally, and purely for the sake of simplicity, we will also assume that the rentals are never increased on any of the properties and there is no capital repayment of any of the mortgages (i.e. we assume that they are all interest-only mortgages).

Example 'D', Part 3
After continuing in the same way for 15 years, Lenny and Dawn will each have a portfolio of six properties.

Lenny's properties now produce total annual rental profits of £23,936. After higher rate Income Tax, this leaves £14,362 of annual after-tax income.

Dawn's property company is now receiving annual rental profits of £31,514, leaving a sum of £26,404 after Corporation Tax.

Let us suppose that at this point both Lenny and Dawn wish to stop reinvesting, retire and start spending their rental profits privately. We already know how much net income Lenny will receive.

For Dawn, we now need to take account of the Income Tax and extra Corporation Tax that she will suffer when she withdraws her profits from the company.

Saunders Limited's effective average Corporation Tax rate before paying any dividends is 16.21%. This means that the additional Corporation Tax charge on the payment of dividends is 2.79%. Dawn may therefore take a dividend of £25,688 (£26,404 times 100/102.79).

After suffering Income Tax on her dividend at an effective rate of 25%, Dawn will therefore be left with net annual income of £19,266.

Analysis of Example 'D', Part 3

What this example shows is that the ability to reinvest a greater share of the annual rental profits over a number of years has ultimately provided Dawn, the corporate investor, with a massively increased income.

The company investor has an after-tax income 34% greater than that enjoyed by the personal investor.

This example has shown that, in a long-term reinvestment scenario, a property investment company really can provide enormous tax benefits to those who build up a portfolio of properties and ultimately use it to generate income.

10.10 Retaining the Wealth

So far, so good, but we still haven't tackled the problem of the different capital gains regime within the company. Although Lenny and Dawn have now stopped reinvesting, they do still have the pressure of a property-letting business to worry about. To genuinely and completely retire, they may, in fact, wish to now sell all of their properties.

To look at the final outcome involved on the ultimate sale of the property portfolios, let's move on one final three-year period and assume that Lenny and Dawn each then sell all of their properties.

We will also need to make three other major assumptions for this purpose:

i)   Property values have increased at an average rate of 5% per annum (compound).

ii) Inflation has averaged 3% per annum.

iii) There have been no changes to the tax system, other than an increase in the annual Capital Gains Tax exemption to £10,000.

Example 'D', Part 4

Eighteen years after we started, Lenny's property portfolio is worth a total of £1,441,765. The total cost of this portfolio was £744,587, thus giving him total capital gains of £647,177. He will be entitled to taper relief at varying rates, as he has held the properties for different periods of time. Overall, his taper relief works out at £240,671, leaving tapered gains of £406,507.

Deducting the annual exemption leaves a taxable gain of £396,507, thus giving rise to a Capital Gains Tax liability (at 40%) of £158,603.

After paying his Capital Gains Tax and also repaying all of his mortgages, Lenny will be left with net proceeds of £901,951.

Now let's look at Dawn.

The property portfolio in Dawn's company will now be worth a total of £1,983,729. The cost of the portfolio was £1,155,405, producing total capital gains of £828,324. Indexation relief will amount to a total of £434,093, leaving taxable indexed gains of £394,231.

To calculate the Corporation Tax on Dawn's company's gains, we would also need to know how much income the company has in the same year.

Let's assume this is the same sum of £31,514 as in Part 3 above.

The Corporation Tax on the company's capital gains is therefore as follows:

- *23.75% on £18,486 (the remainder of the second effective Corporation Tax rate band available),*

- *19% on £250,000, and*

- *32.75% on £125,745.*

Total Corporation Tax = £93,072.

After paying this Corporation Tax and repaying all of the mortgages which the company took out, the remaining funds in the company will be £1,256,874. Dawn now has to wind up Saunders Limited in order to get these proceeds into her own hands. Here, we will assume that she originally invested £250,000 in the company (the value of her first property), meaning that she will have a capital gain of £1,006,874. (We are again ignoring the costs of the winding up as we did in section 10.7.)

Dawn is entitled to 40% taper relief on this gain, as well as her annual exemption of £10,000, leaving her with a taxable gain of £594,124. Her Capital Gains Tax on the winding up of her property investment company will therefore amount to £237,650, leaving her with net proceeds of £1,019,224.

Analysis of Example 'D', Part 4

So how much better off is the company investor compared with the private investor?

Ultimately, our corporate investor, Dawn, has emerged some £117,273, or 13%, better off than Lenny, our personal investor.

Although this gap is not as wide as that on the net <u>income</u> shown in Part 3 above, it does indicate that reinvestment of the additional net income receivable though the use of a company should eventually produce a sufficiently improved position to compensate for the disadvantages of realising capital gains in, and extracting them from, a company.

10.11 Long-term Reinvestment Conclusions

After taking a long and detailed look at the probable outcomes for two investors over many years, (one corporate and one personal), we can still see that the fundamental position remains that companies are a good vehicle in which to build a portfolio, but do tend to suffer some drawbacks on its eventual disposal.

However, the example does show that the accumulation and reinvestment of additional net profits within a company over many years will eventually produce a beneficial result, even after taking the capital gains position into account.

In reality, things will not be exactly as we have predicted here. It is impossible to generalise the true position for every single property investor's likely outcome. Investors must therefore consider their own plans and their own view of the probable outcome in order to decide how this illustration best applies to them.

Chapter 11

How to Set Up Your Own Property Company

11.1 Who Can Help & How Much Does it Cost?

If you do decide to go ahead and form a property company, it is pretty easy to do. Most lawyers can form a company for you, as well as many accountants. Some have so-called 'off the shelf' companies available for use at a moment's notice.

Alternatively, if you feel confident about tackling the paperwork yourself, there are specialist company formation agents you can use, which will work out cheaper than using another intermediary. The typical cost of forming a company through a formation agent is around £150. If you use a lawyer or accountant to assist with the task, however, the costs may well be more.

A UK company can be registered in Scotland, in Northern Ireland or in England and Wales. An odd little quirk arises from the fact that, since the main branch of Companies House for England and Wales is actually in Cardiff, one could say that these companies are in fact registered in Wales.

From 8th October 2004, it will also be possible to form a 'Societas Europaea' (or "SE" for short), a new form of European company being introduced throughout the European Union. The tax treatment of a 'Societas Europaea' will depend entirely on where it is resident and hence if you form one of these new companies and base it in the UK, it will be subject to Corporation Tax in exactly the same way as any other UK company.

11.2 The Company's Constitution

The company will need a constitution. This is embodied in two documents:

- The company's Memorandum of Association, and

- The company's Articles of Association

The Memorandum covers what the company is empowered to do and sets out the framework for its share structure. Most modern Memorandums of Association empower the company to do pretty much anything. For a property company, it is important to ensure that the company has the power to:

- Borrow money,

- Buy or sell land and property, and

- Rent out, or grant lease over, property

As well as anything else that you are expecting to need the company to do.

The Articles of Association govern the rights of the holders of each class of shares (there only needs to be one class, but there can be more), as well as the power to appoint (or remove) directors or auditors (where necessary) and the conduct of general meetings of the company's members.

Most sets of Articles will refer to a sort of 'default' set of rules known as 'Table A', which is published as part of the Companies Act. You can, however, have different rules for your company if you wish (within the boundaries of Company Law).

A company can either be a private company or a public limited company (PLC). Most companies are private companies and there is little point in being a PLC unless you are seeking a stock-market quotation. A PLC must have a company seal. For private companies this is optional and is quite rare nowadays.

You will need to appoint at least two people as 'officers' of the company. Officers include directors and the company secretary. Your company must have one company secretary and at least one director. If there is only one director, that person cannot also be the company secretary (hence why there must be at least two officers).

If you use a company formation agent, you will find that they ask a great many questions about the prospective officers of the company nowadays for the sake of 'security'. This is all in the name of the 'money laundering' regulations. Details requested have been known to include eye colour, mother's maiden name and certain digits from National Insurance numbers.

The company will need a registered office address, which must be occupied and cannot be a mere P.O. box. The company's name should be displayed prominently at the registered address and its statutory books and records should be kept there.

To begin with, the company's accounting date will be set as the date falling 12 months after the end of the month in which the company is first registered. As explained in section 11.3 below, however, the accounting date can easily be changed.

The owners of shares in the company are referred to as 'members'. A company must have at least one member (some years ago, there had to be at least two).

Shortly after you register your company with Companies House you will receive a letter from them congratulating you on your new company and advising you of some of your responsibilities as a company director.

You will also receive a form CT41G from the Inland Revenue. Don't panic, but don't ignore it either. You should complete and return the CT41G in order to get the company into the Corporation Tax system. It is vital that you do this within three months of when the company commences any business activities. Penalties will be imposed if you do not return the completed form within this timescale.

Of more immediate concern will be the need to register the company as an employer for PAYE purposes or for VAT, if either of these are applicable.

Once you have your company, it can go ahead and borrow money or purchase new properties without too much difficulty (provided the lenders are willing to co-operate!).

11.3 Changing Your Company's Accounting Date

Note that a company's accounting year-end date does not need to remain the same date permanently and can generally be changed by notifying Companies House in advance of the earlier of:

a) The new desired date, or
b) The first anniversary of the previous accounting year-end date.

There are, however, limits on how often such changes may be made and it is not possible (nor, most likely, desirable), to keep 'playing around' with the company's year end date on a regular basis. Nevertheless, it remains safe to say that any company may change its accounting date to any date it chooses at least once.

Naturally, where a change is made to the accounting date, for whatever reason, the company will have a short or long accounting period (i.e. a period other than a year), which will be dealt with in the manner explained in Appendix D.

Wealth Warning

As explained in Appendix D, longer accounting periods give rise to two periods for Corporation Tax purposes. In the case of very long accounting periods, the Corporation Tax payable for the first twelve months of the accounting period will be due very shortly after, or, in the most extreme cases, even before, the end of the accounting period. This gives rise to practical problems in calculating the amount of tax due in time to make the Corporation Tax payment and can inevitably lead to either:

i)   Overpayments which take some months to recoup, or

ii)   Underpayments which give rise to interest costs.

Chapter 12

How to Put Existing Property into a Company

12.1 Introduction

The basic problem with transferring anything into your company is the fact that you and the company are 'connected'. As explained in section 5.2, this means that any transfers of assets between you and the company will be deemed to take place at market value for Capital Gains Tax purposes.

Potentially, therefore, you could face a huge Capital Gains Tax bill if you try to transfer existing properties into a company. How big this tax bill is will depend on the type of property business you have.

12.2 'Trading' Businesses

If your business is regarded as 'trading' for tax purposes (see Chapter Three), there are two specific Capital Gains Tax reliefs that are available to alleviate this problem:

- Relief for 'Gifts Of Business Assets', and

- So-called 'Incorporation Relief'.

Where the underlying business being carried on qualifies for one of these reliefs, the relief is equally available to transferor individuals, partnerships or trusts. However, for the rest of this section, I will refer just to individual transferors for the sake of simplicity.

Wealth Warning

When considering the transfer of a whole property business in order to obtain the relevant Capital Gains Tax relief, it is important to remember that there will also be other tax issues involved.

Such a transfer will be regarded as a cessation of trade for Income Tax purposes. It will also be necessary to make appropriate elections relating to trading stock, development work-in-progress and capital allowances, in order to prevent unwanted and unnecessary tax liabilities from arising.

Gifts of Business Assets

The first of the two potential reliefs available for 'trading' businesses is something of a misnomer, since, in fact, the relief generally will only apply to trading assets, rather than what the average taxpayer would regard as a business asset. Within tax legislation, 'business' is a much wider term than 'trade' and, as we have discussed already, property investment or property letting is not usually considered to be a 'trade' for tax purposes.

The relief for 'Gifts Of Business Assets' works where you actually 'gift' your property business to your company for no consideration, or perhaps for a consideration that is low enough to ensure that no Capital Gains Tax is payable.

The relief works by allowing the capital gain which arises on the transfer under the normal rules to be 'held over'. This means that the individual making the transfer has no Capital Gains Tax liability, but it also means that the assets transferred to the company have a lower base cost (see section 5.3). The assets' base cost is reduced by the amount of gain 'held over'. The gain 'held over' for these purposes is the untapered gain, meaning that any accumulated taper relief on the assets transferred at this point is effectively lost.

Note that this relief is not automatic and a claim must be made jointly by the transferring taxpayer and the recipient company. Under self-assessment, the claim must be made using the form provided with helpsheet IR295 (obtainable from the usual Inland Revenue orderline or website – see Appendix F).

The relief cannot be used to transfer shares in one company from an individual's ownership into the ownership of another company.

Example
Tom runs a property development business from his office in Glasgow. He decides that he would like to transfer the whole business, including his office, into a new company, Smith Developments Limited.

Tom bought his office for £100,000 in March 2000 and has used it as his trading premises ever since. Its current market value is £250,000, but Tom 'gifts' the property (i.e. transfers it for no consideration) to Smith Developments Limited in March 2005.

Under the normal rules, Tom would have had a capital gain of £150,000 before taper relief. However, if Tom and his company jointly elect to 'hold over' the gain, Tom will have no chargeable capital gain. Smith Developments Limited's base cost in the office property will be its market value, £250,000, less the 'held over' gain of £150,000, i.e. £100,000.

In this example, the company has ended up with the same base cost for the office property as the individual owner had. This will generally be the case for assets originally acquired by the individual transferor after March 1998. For older assets, however, the impact of indexation relief will complicate maters a little.

Note that Tom's actual capital gain (had he not elected to 'hold over') would have been reduced by taper relief at 75% and possibly also his annual exemption (if available). His actual potential Capital Gains Tax bill may have been as low as £5,658.

Against this, we must weigh the fact that a sale of the property by the company after the transfer would give rise to a Corporation Tax bill of at least £28,500 (depending on the level of the company's income).

It's a case of a small amount of tax now versus a much greater amount of potential tax in the future. Tough call!

Tax Tip

Rather than 'gifting' assets to the company for no consideration, it is often worth selling them for a small sum in order to utilise the transferor individual's available reliefs.

The 'Gifts Of Business Assets' relief can still be used to 'hold over' the element of the gain which arises only due to the 'deemed' sale proceeds at market value rule, with the individual's Capital Gains Tax calculation then proceeding on the basis of the actual consideration.

With many new companies, this is often done by agreeing a sale price for the asset and allowing that sum to be left outstanding as a loan from the transferor to the company.

The loan may be paid back to the transferor as the company's funds permit, giving him what is, to all practical intents and purposes, a tax-free income from the company until his loan is paid off.

Example Revisited

In the above example, Tom could have transferred the office property to Smith Developments Limited for £132,800. After electing to 'hold over' the amount representing the difference between market value and actual consideration (£117,600), this would leave him with a capital gain of £32,800.

After taper relief at 75%, Tom's gain is reduced to £8,200 and this is then covered by his annual Capital Gains Tax exemption, leaving him with no tax to pay and a 'tax-free' sum of £32,800 which he can draw upon as funds permit.

Meanwhile, Smith Developments Limited's base cost is £32,800 more than it would have been and this will save at least £6,232 in Corporation Tax on a sale of the property (possibly as much as £10,742).

Incorporation Relief

This other relief is also generally only available for transfers of 'trading' businesses (as explained in Chapter Three). (But see below for its possible application to property-investment businesses.)

It works along similar principles to the relief for 'Gifts Of Business Assets', except that:

- The transferor individual must transfer the whole of the business as a 'going concern'.

- The transfer must be wholly or partly in exchange for shares in the transferee company (the relief will only apply to the part of the sale consideration which is satisfied in shares).

- The gain 'held over' is deducted from the transferor individual's base cost in the shares and not from the underlying assets transferred. In effect, this means that the transferor's Capital Gains Tax base cost for those shares is the same as the base cost which they had for all of the underlying assets prior to the transfer.

- Where the necessary conditions apply, the relief is given automatically. However, for business transfers after 5th April 2002, the transferor may elect to disapply the relief. (Why would they want to disapply it? – see the warning below.)

Wealth Warning

Incorporation relief will eliminate, or at least reduce, the Capital Gains Tax arising on the transfer of an individual's qualifying business to a company.

However, it is essential to remember that this will mean that the taper relief 'clock' is reset at zero.

In other words, even if the owner has had the business for many years, for taper relief purposes, any subsequent sale of the new company's shares will be dealt with on the basis that the owner only acquired the business asset at the date that those shares were received.

This is why it is sometimes better to disapply this relief.

An election to disapply incorporation relief must normally be made by the second anniversary of the 31st January after the tax year in which the transfer took place.

E.g. transfer during 2004/2005: deadline to elect to disapply = 31st January 2008.

However, if the transferor has disposed of all of the shares received as consideration for the transfer by the end of the next tax year after the transfer, the deadline is accelerated by a year.

E.g. transfer during 2004/2005, all consideration shares sold by 5th April 2006: deadline to disapply = 31st January 2007.

Example
Chris has run a property development business for many years. In December 2004, he transfers the business to Paterson Developments Limited in exchange for shares in the company.

Chris' business had a market value of £1,000,000 at the time of the transfer and he had a base cost of £14,000. Chris is a higher rate taxpayer and hence, without incorporation relief he would have a Capital Gains Tax liability of £95,320 (after taking account of taper relief at 75% and his annual exemption of £8,200).

In July 2005, Chris receives an offer of £1,200,000 for his company and decides to sell.

As Chris had only held the shares in his company for seven months, he is not entitled to any taper relief on this sale. Worse still, his base cost in the shares appears to be only £14,000 due to the operation of incorporation relief. This would give him a Capital Gains Tax liability of £471,000! (Based on an estimated annual exemption of £8,500 for 2005/2006, in case you're checking my arithmetic.)

Fortunately, Chris has until 31st January 2007 to elect to disapply incorporation relief.

This will reinstate his 2004/2005 Capital Gains Tax liability of £95,320, but will reduce his liability on the sale of the shares during 2005/2006 to only £76,600 (as the base cost of the shares will now be £1,000,000).

Chris' total Capital Gains Tax bill for both transactions will now be only £171,920, a saving of £299,080!

Tax Tip

To preserve the normal deadline for the election to disapply, make sure that you don't sell all of the shares you receive on the transfer. You simply need to hang on to a handful of them until after the end of the next tax year in order to preserve the original deadline – in case you need more time to work out your best option.

12.3 Furnished Holiday Lettings

As usual, furnished holiday lettings businesses (see section 4.5) have a privileged status and transfers of such businesses are eligible for both the relief for 'Gifts Of Business Assets' and Incorporation Relief.

12.4 Property Investment Businesses

The relief for 'Gifts Of Business Assets' is now strictly restricted to businesses which also qualify as 'trading' for taper relief purposes.

A property investment business will therefore never be eligible for that relief.

The requirements for Incorporation Relief are not quite so strict and only require a 'business' rather than a 'trade'. However, some of the case law on the subject states that the "mere passive holding of investments and collection of rent does not amount to a business" for this purpose.

Hence, whether Incorporation Relief might be available for a property investment business remains uncertain. It will be necessary to take a very detailed look at the individual circumstances before deciding whether Incorporation Relief might possibly be available. It might be possible to claim the relief where the owner has a well-established business and is actively involved in the day-to-day running of it, so that the Inland Revenue could not say that the properties were mere 'passive' investments.

Nevertheless, as I say, the position remains uncertain and I would not like to rely on a claim for Incorporation Relief for any property investment business other than a furnished holiday lettings business.

What Does This Leave?

Without the availability of any special Capital Gains Tax relief, the owner of investment properties faces the problem of separate capital gains calculations on the transfer of each individual property. In each case, the owner faces a Capital Gains Tax bill based on a 'deemed' sale at market value.

Sometimes, with careful timing and the use of annual exemptions, taper relief, etc, it is, however, still possible to make the transfers at little or no tax cost.

The possible availability of Principal Private Residence relief on some properties should also be borne in mind when considering this type of strategy. (But see section 14.2 regarding private use of property after putting it into a company.)

Tax Tip

A former Principal Private Residence may usually be transferred tax-free into a property investment company at any time up until at least three years after it ceases to be your main residence (and possibly much later in some circumstances).

Be careful, however, if the property was not always your main residence throughout the period from purchase up until when you finally moved out of it.

However, generally speaking, it remains difficult to get an existing property investment business into a company without running the risk of incurring a large Capital Gains Tax bill.

In most cases, therefore, it is safer to look to the company as a vehicle only for your future investments and to keep your existing properties in your own hands.

The 'Backdoor Route'

Borrowings secured on your existing personal property portfolio could be invested in the company to enable it to acquire new property. You, in turn, would be eligible for Income Tax relief on the interest on such borrowings, as the funds are being invested in a 'Close Company' (see section 14.1).

Another Possibility

One other possibility that might be worth exploring in these circumstances is the use of a property management company (see section 14.5).

Chapter 13

Borrowing Money the Tax-efficient Way

13.1 Introduction

A property company that borrows to finance property purchases or other aspects of its property business gets relief for interest and other finance costs in the same way as an individual property investor.

Investors themselves will obtain tax relief for interest on borrowings invested in the property company, provided that it is a 'Close Company', but not classed as a 'Close Investment Holding Company'. Both of these terms are explained in section 14.1.

To obtain relief, the investor must also either have a 'material interest' in the company, or must hold <u>some</u> ordinary shares in the company <u>and</u> work for the greater part of their time in the actual conduct or management of the company's business.

A 'material interest' is broadly defined as more than 5% of the company's share capital and shares held by 'connected' persons (see Appendix B) may be counted for this purpose, as long as the individual concerned does hold some of the shares personally.

In most cases, the investor will qualify as having a 'material interest', although, for a large property company, it may be that some new investors come on board who qualify for relief through the second criterion instead.

The investor is equally eligible for interest relief on funds borrowed to purchase shares in the company or to lend to the company.

13.2 Who Should Borrow the Funds?

When investing in property through a company, there are three possible approaches to the financing structure:

i) Borrow the funds personally and then invest them in shares in the company.

ii) Borrow the funds personally and then lend them to the company.

iii) Borrow the funds within the company.

These three different structures make several important differences to the overall tax situation:

a) Tax relief on the interest paid.

b) Additional tax arising due to the need to extract funds to service personal debt held outside the company.

c) The Capital Gains Tax position on an ultimate winding up or sale of the company.

d) Stamp Duty on a sale of the company's shares.

They do not, however, make any difference to the capital gains position on property disposals made by the company itself.

An additional non-tax issue is the impact on the investor's ability to withdraw the sums invested back out of the company.

Let's now take a look at the implications of each structure in turn (we are assuming here that the company is a Close Company but not a Close Investment Holding Company):

13.3 Borrowing to Invest in Shares

The individual will obtain interest relief on the borrowings. If the individual is a higher rate taxpayer, this will, at first glance, generally appear to be advantageous, as relief is being given at a higher effective rate than it would have been had the interest been borne by the company itself.

If the individual is able to service the debt from other resources then this is all well and good. However, in most cases, it will be necessary to extract funds from the company in order to service the debt.

Example
Gill, a higher rate taxpayer, borrowed £100,000 to invest in her own property company. She pays annual interest totalling £7,000, thus providing her with effective relief of £2,800 (at 40%).

However, in order to pay this interest, Gill has to take a dividend of £7,000 out of her company. This costs her an additional £1,750 (25%) in Income Tax meaning that her effective relief for the interest is only £1,050 (15%).

Clearly, if personal debt needs to be serviced through the withdrawal of funds from the company, this will generally eliminate any apparent advantage of obtaining interest relief personally. The situation would be further exacerbated if the company also incurs an additional Corporation Tax charge on the dividend payments (see section 2.3).

Note that we have only considered the payment of interest here and have ignored capital repayments. These would, of course, only serve to further increase the Income Tax cost on the withdrawal of the necessary funds from the company.

In our example, Gill was a higher rate taxpayer. Other taxpayers would not have the problem of Income Tax arising on the sums withdrawn from the company by way of dividend. Their position will therefore depend on the marginal Corporation Tax rate being paid by the company (see section 2.2).

In other words, this financial structure would produce better tax relief on interest than in section 13.5 below whenever the non-higher rate taxpayer individual is paying Income Tax at a higher rate than the company's marginal Corporation Tax rate.

Wealth Warning

Beware though, when applying the principle set out above, that the effective marginal Corporation Tax rate on distributed profits will now always be at least 19%.

However, the problem, of course, with entering a financing structure that is beneficial for you as a non-higher rate taxpayer, is that you may find yourself still stuck with it after you have become a higher rate taxpayer and the structure that you have is therefore no longer beneficial.

On a winding up under this structure, the individual will have a high base cost in the company's shares, thus reducing the potential Capital Gains Tax impact (as was the case for Louise in Example 'C', Part 3 in section 10.7).

A sale of the company's shares could give rise to a fairly substantial Stamp Duty bill for the purchaser, as much of its value will be held as non-distributable share capital.

Another big drawback to this structure is the difficulty in withdrawing the funds invested. This requires a winding up, corporate restructuring or company purchase of own shares. We have covered winding up in section 10.7. While in some cases they can prove worthwhile, the other possible methods are likely to prove costly in terms of both the tax charges arising and the professional fees that will be incurred.

13.4 Borrowing to Lend to the Company

Lending funds to the company will produce the same interest relief as in section 13.3 above, as long as the loan is structured properly. All of the same issues regarding withdrawal of the necessary funds, etc, apply here in equal measure.

On a winding up, the amounts due to the investor can be repaid without any tax implications. This would leave the same level of Capital Gains Tax as in section 13.3 above.

However, on a sale of the company, these funds would effectively be deducted from the value of the company's shares, thus reducing the amount of Stamp Duty payable by the purchaser.

The big advantage of this structure (over section 13.3) is that the funds invested can be withdrawn from the company at any time (with no tax liability), if the cash is available.

Furthermore, the investor can, if desired, also charge the company interest on the outstanding loan from them to the company. Provided that the interest charged does not exceed a commercial rate, the company will obtain Corporation Tax relief, although the investor will, of course, be taxed on this income (at the 'savings' rate – see Appendix C). This is sometimes a useful third alternative for 'profit extraction' (see section 8.2), as Corporation Tax relief is obtained without any National Insurance costs arising.

13.5 Corporate Borrowings

Where the company obtains funds through its own direct borrowings, this will, of course, mean that it is the company which claims relief for the interest costs. However, it also means that there will be no need to extract funds from the company in order to service the debt.

Whether this is better or worse than the position in section 13.3 will depend on whether the investor would have had to withdraw funds from the company to service any private debt, as well as the marginal Corporation Tax rate being paid by the company and the individual investor's own tax position.

In a case like Gill's (our higher rate taxpayer from the previous example), borrowings in the company would produce a better overall effective result for interest relief.

The position on a winding up under this type of structure will depend on whether the borrowings are still in place at that time. If, at that time, there are still loans to be repaid out of property disposals, then the total sums to be distributed on the winding up will be reduced.

Hence, if all of the borrowings were still in place, the position would again be much the same as in Example 'C', Part 3 in section 10.7.

However, if the borrowings have been repaid, this means that the sum distributed on the winding up is increased.

Example 'C', Part 4

Returning to our earlier example, (sections 10.6 and 10.7), let us now suppose that Louise set Dawson Limited up with only a small nominal sum in share capital (so small, in fact, that we will ignore it altogether for the sake of illustration). Dawson Limited borrowed £250,000 to finance the property purchase and these borrowings have now been completely repaid out of rent received by the company.

The net property disposal proceeds of £466,750 will therefore be distributed to Louise on the winding up (once more ignoring professional fees incurred, etc). Again, this represents a capital disposal by Louise but, this time, she has no (or very little) base cost to set off. She will therefore have a tapered gain of £280,050. Even after deducting her 2013/2014 annual exemption of £10,000, her taxable gain will be £270,050.

Louise's Capital Gains Tax on this gain will be between £101,538 and £108,020, meaning that the total tax burden on this property disposal would be between £134,788 and £141,270! (The Corporation Tax paid by Dawson Limited on the property sale was £33,250.)

Analysis of Example 'C', Part 4

Clearly, this is the worst result of all for Louise, indicating quite strongly that this financing structure (corporate borrowings) can have severe financial drawbacks.

This situation has arisen because Louise has used the company's rental profits to repay its borrowings rather than extract them from the company. In section 10.5, we saw that this was a good strategy for a property company from an income perspective. However, in this example, we can see that it has only led to problems at a later stage. Inevitably, this result is bound to arise where the eventual intention is to realise gains and extract the proceeds from the company for personal use.

From a Stamp Duty perspective, this structure is similar to section 13.4 above while the borrowings remain in place, but more akin to section 13.3 above when the borrowings have been repaid (i.e. high value in shares producing high Stamp Duty for a purchaser).

Since, under this structure, the investor/shareholder does not really invest any significant sums in the company, the question of withdrawing the original investment does not arise in this case. However, from Example 'C', Part 4, it is quite clear that any profits that are not withdrawn can lead to problems later!

Nevertheless, we must contrast this outcome with the position that arose in Example 'D' in sections 10.9 and 10.10, where we saw that the accumulation of additional after-tax resources could eventually compensate for the greater tax burden on the ultimate capital gains.

As usual, it is for individual investors to weigh up the conflicting factors in order to decide which approach is best for them.

Of course, in practice, the investor does not always have the luxury of being able to choose what financing structure is wanted, as banks will very often only be prepared to lend to the individual person.

Chapter 14

Some Important Tax Issues

14.1 Close vs Close Investment Holding Companies

Broadly speaking, a private company is a 'Close Company' if it is under the control of five or fewer persons. 'Control' is based on voting power vested in share capital held by those persons. Shares held by 'connected' persons (see Appendix B) are included when considering the application of this rule.

As complex as the above definition may seem, what it means is that the vast majority of private property companies will be Close Companies for tax purposes.

Nowadays, this represents good news, as additional reliefs are available in respect of shares and other investments in Close Companies (including interest relief – see Chapter Thirteen) although, in the past, being a Close Company had distinct disadvantages.

Close Investment Holding Companies

A close company will be a Close Investment Holding Company unless it exists wholly or mainly for one or more 'qualifying purposes'. 'Qualifying purposes' include carrying on a trade and "making investments in land let, or intended to be let, other than to connected persons".

Hence, a property business will generally represent a qualifying purpose and a property company will <u>not</u>, therefore, usually be a Close Investment Holding Company.

This is very important because Close Investment Holding Companies must pay Corporation Tax at the **main rate** (30%) on all of their profits and gains. Furthermore, investors are not eligible for interest relief for investments in Close Investment Holding Companies.

Most property companies, however, do remain eligible for the full range of effective Corporation Tax rates set out in section 2.2 and their investors are eligible for interest relief, as explained in Chapter Thirteen (but see section 14.2).

14.2 Tax Dangers of Private Use

It is generally not advisable to hold properties through a company where there is some private use. For these purposes, 'private use' would include:

- Using it as your own private residence (whether or not your main residence).

- Allowing your spouse or any other member of your family to use it as a private residence.

- Letting the property to any 'connected' person.

Private use of a property held through a company could result in:

- The company becoming a Close Investment Holding Company and therefore having to pay the main rate of Corporation Tax on **all** profits.

- Loss of interest relief on sums invested in the company.

- Loss of taper relief on company shares (where they might otherwise qualify as a 'business asset').

- Income Tax Benefit in Kind charges on the company's directors.

- Class 1A National Insurance liabilities for the company.

- Deemed distributions of income which are taxable on the shareholders as if they were dividends.

Furthermore, where a property owned personally does have private use, there is scope to make use of the Principal Private Residence exemption, Private Letting Relief and Rent-a-Room relief. The scope to use these reliefs is lost if the property is held in a company.

In short, **DON'T DO IT!**

14.3 Selling the Company the Tax-efficient Way

Very often a property company will continue in the same ownership (or at least the same family) until its usefulness has expired, when it will be wound up. We looked at this in section 10.7. Sometimes, however, a property company may be sold with its existing business intact. This is particularly likely when the purchaser wishes to acquire a whole ready-made portfolio.

The sale of the company represents a capital disposal and the individual investor making the sale will therefore have a Capital Gains Tax liability in much the same way as that arising on a winding up.

Example
Isabel started her property-investment company, Angel Limited, in 1999 with an investment of just £10,000 share capital.

In 2010, she decides to sell the whole company to Big Properties PLC for £1,000,000. Her capital gain on the sale is therefore £990,000. After taper relief at 40% (more than 10 years ownership, non-business taper rate applies), she is left with a tapered gain of £594,000. Deducting her annual exemption of, say, £9,500, leaves a taxable gain of £584,500, on which she will pay Capital Gains Tax of between £227,318 and £233,800 (at 2004/2005 rates), depending on her level of income for that tax year.

Tax Tip

Note that the rate of taper relief that Isabel may claim is based on how long she has owned the <u>company</u> and not on how long she has owned any of the individual properties within the company. This means that the company provides a vehicle within which the property portfolio may be developed and changed over a number of years with no consequent loss of taper relief for the investor.

Stamp Duty

A huge advantage for the purchaser of a property company is the ability to make large Stamp Duty savings, as only 0.5% will need to be paid on the purchase price of the shares. Not only is this considerably less than the Stamp Duty Land Tax rate of up to 4% applying to property purchases, but also, as explained in section 13.4, the actual amount of consideration to which the duty applies may also sometimes be reduced.

Given the commercial advantages of acquiring an existing, well-run property portfolio and the potential Stamp Duty savings, a well-packaged property company can be a very attractive target for potential purchasers. Naturally, one can expect this to be reflected in the sale price!

14.4 Benefits & Dangers of Multiple Companies

"Great," you might be thinking. "I'll form one company for every property and make £10,000 tax-free profit every year in each one!"

Sorry, no, that won't work. In fact, in many cases it would be absolutely disastrous!

This is because all of the Corporation Tax profit bands and limits described in section 2.2 must be divided up where there are any associated companies. The bands are divided equally between all of the relevant associated companies, meaning that the more companies you have, the higher your effective rates of Corporation Tax in each company are going to be.

What is an associated company?

An associated company is another company under the control of the same persons and <u>their</u> associates. (A person's associates are other persons with whom they are 'connected' – see Appendix B.)

Hence, in the simplest case, if you form two companies and own all of the shares in both of them, then these companies are associated with each other.

Exceptions

- A company does not need to be counted as an associated company if it is not carrying on a business. (The term 'business' is defined very widely here and might include, for example, a company holding a portfolio of stock-exchange investments. However, a company that simply had an interest-bearing bank account, and no other assets, has been held <u>not</u> to be carrying on a business for this purpose.)

- Companies that are controlled by relatives other than spouses and minor children do not need to be counted as associated companies unless there is substantial commercial interdependence between the companies.

Subject to the above exceptions, however, <u>any</u> associated company must be taken into account, regardless of what country it is based in or registered in and regardless of what kind of business it is carrying on.

Example

Tina has a property company, Turner One Limited, which makes annual profits of £20,000. Under the current Corporation Tax regime, Turner One Limited's annual Corporation Tax bill is therefore £2,375 (£10,000 @ Nil & £10,000 @ 23.75%).

Tina's property business is expanding, so she decides to form a second company, Turner Two Limited. In its first year, the new company only makes a profit of £1,000. Because there are two associated companies here, the Corporation Tax profit bands and limits must be divided in two.

Each of Tina's companies therefore gets half of the relevant tax bands.

Turner One Limited's Corporation Tax bill is therefore now £3,562.50 (£15,000 @ 23.75% - only £5,000 now falls into the Nil tax rate band).

Turner Two Limited's profits are tax free, as they fall wholly within its £5,000 Nil tax rate band.

If Tina had kept her whole property business in just one company, its Corporation Tax liability would have been £2,612.50 (£10,000 @ Nil & £11,000 @ 23.75%).

The second company has therefore cost Tina an extra £950 in Corporation Tax.

The moral here is that a proliferation of companies is generally a bad idea. As with everything in tax, though, there are exceptions!

Trading Companies

It should be noted that <u>any</u> associated company carrying on <u>any</u> kind of business will have this same effect on the Corporation Tax rates applying to your property company. This remains the case even if your other company carries on an entirely different kind of business.

Conversely, of course, the creation of a property company will have an equally detrimental effect on the Corporation Tax position of any existing trading company which you might have.

You might be tempted, therefore, to think that it would be a good idea to make your property investments through another existing company (thus avoiding the kind of problems which Tina experienced in the example above).

Here again though, great care needs to be exercised. If your other company is carrying on the type of business which is regarded as a 'trade' within the UK tax system, your shares in that company will be eligible for 'business asset' taper relief (see section 6.3). Putting non-qualifying property investments into such a company would jeopardise the 'business asset' status of your shares in that company and could eventually cost you dearly in Capital Gains Tax!

In this type of scenario, you would need to weigh your annual Corporation Tax costs against your eventual Capital Gains Tax position in order to determine the best course of action overall.

Generally, I would tend to suggest that you should avoid tainting a trading company whose shares qualify as 'business assets', as this is a very valuable relief. This, therefore, is an exception where the use of an additional company is advisable.

14.5 Property Management Companies

We have looked at the taxation status of property management companies a few times throughout this guide and it is now worth taking a look at how these companies might be used as a planning tool.

The objective of this type of planning is to reduce the tax burden on the income from your properties without having the problems inherent in putting the properties themselves into a company.

The principle is best illustrated (as so often) by way of an example.

Example
Jonah has a large property portfolio generating annual gross rents of £200,000 and a taxable profit of £50,000. He is a higher rate taxpayer and hence pays £20,000 in Income Tax each year on these profits.

He now decides to sub-contract the management of his properties to a new property management company, Lomu Property Services Limited.

Lomu Property Services Limited charges Jonah 15% of the gross annual rents on the properties (£30,000) as a service charge for managing the portfolio. Naturally, the company also ends up bearing some of the expenses in running the property portfolio and these amount to £5,000.

Jonah will now have a taxable annual rental income of £25,000 (£50,000, as before, less the £30,000 service charges from

Lomu Property Services Limited, but add back the costs of £5,000 now borne by the company). This reduces his annual Income Tax bill to £10,000.

Meanwhile, Lomu Property Services Limited will have an annual profit chargeable to Corporation Tax of £25,000 (the £30,000 service charge less £5,000 expenses). The company's annual Corporation Tax bill will therefore amount to £3,563 (£15,000 at 23.75% - the first £10,000 of profit is tax free).

The total annual tax paid by Jonah and Lomu Property Services Limited is £13,563, which is £6,437 less than before. (A saving of over 32%!)

As usual, it doesn't work quite so well if the company's profits are extracted. If Jonah takes the maximum amount of after-tax profit out of the company as a dividend, he will have additional Income Tax of £5,116 to pay and the company will have an additional Corporation Tax liability of £972, leaving him only £349 better off than when he started.

Wealth Warning

This type of arrangement is likely to attract close Inland Revenue scrutiny and it is essential to ensure that the commercial reality of the situation matches up to the tax planning.

Firstly, the amount of service charge levied by the company must not exceed a normal commercial rate for those services.

Secondly, for Jonah to be able to claim a valid Income Tax deduction for these charges, he must be able to show that they were incurred wholly and exclusively for the benefit of his property rental business. In other words, there must be a genuine provision of services by the company.

Thirdly, the company itself must be carrying on a trade on a commercial basis. Otherwise, the company would be classed as a Close Investment Holding Company and most of the potential tax saving would be lost. To satisfy this requirement, the company should be managing other properties as well and not just those of the owner.

The arrangement will work best if there is a full-blown property management business, managing properties for a number of unconnected landlords on a fully commercial arm's length basis.

The service charges levied on the owner's property business from the company should be on the same basis as those for other landlords using the same services.

Tax Tip

Subject to the points set out above, even greater tax savings may be possible if the property management company is owned by and/or employs the investor's spouse or other adult family members.

14.6 Commercial Investment Properties

Since 6th April 2000, commercial property (i.e. non-residential) let to an unquoted trading company has qualified as a 'business asset' for Capital Gains Tax taper relief purposes, meaning that 75% taper relief would be available on a sale of such property after two years or more.

From 6th April 2004, this treatment is being extended to all commercial property let to any qualifying business. This will cover many types of property, such as offices, shops, workshops, factories, etc, and will eventually mean that 75% taper relief will be available after two years on almost all non-residential property.

This has major implications for the decision on whether to use a property company and, if you are in the business of letting out, or investing in, commercial property, you will need to take this into account.

Remember, companies do not get taper relief!

Furthermore, although most commercial properties owned personally will soon be getting the higher 'business asset' rate of taper relief, this does not alter the fact that shares in a property investment company will continue to be classed as 'non-business assets', even if the company's underlying business is that of letting out commercial property.

While there will inevitably be some exceptions, this does lead to the conclusion that commercial investment properties should probably not now be put into a company.

14.7 Becoming Non Resident

Throughout this guide, we have been looking at the implications for UK Resident property investors using a UK Resident property company. Space does not permit a detailed examination of the position for non-residents, but it is worth making a few brief observations.

Tax Residence for Companies

Subject to any applicable Double Tax Treaty, a company is treated as UK Resident if:

i)   It is UK Registered, or

ii)   It has its place of central management and control in the UK.

A detailed examination of (ii) would take too long to fit in here, but it is fair to say that if you are UK Resident, it is very difficult for any property company which you run not to be regarded as UK Resident also.

Emigration for Companies

Generally speaking, a UK Registered company cannot 'emigrate' – i.e. it cannot cease to be UK Resident. This may, however, in some cases, be overridden by the terms of a Double Tax Treaty between the UK and another country.

If a UK Resident company does succeed in 'emigrating', i.e. becoming non-UK Resident, then, unless it does so with the specific consent of Her Majesty's Treasury, it must pay an 'exit charge'. The 'exit charge' is basically a sum equal to the Corporation Tax that would arise if the company were to sell all of its assets at their market value.

In view of these points, any UK Resident individual who ultimately intends to emigrate should think very carefully before using a property company.

Non-resident Companies

In the same way as for non-resident individuals, subject to any applicable Double Tax Treaty, a non-UK resident company is liable for UK tax on income from UK property, but is exempt from tax on capital gains unless connected with trading activities in the UK.

However, if a non-Resident company is under the control of a UK Resident individual, then the individual is liable for Capital Gains Tax on the capital gains made by that company.

Hence, overseas (non-Resident) companies are of little use to UK Resident individual investors.

Even for non-UK Resident individuals investing in UK property, the situation is not exactly clear-cut.

Wealth Warning

If attempting to run a UK property portfolio through an overseas company, it is essential to ensure that the company's 'place of central management and control' is outwith the UK.

Otherwise, the company will be deemed to be UK Resident, thus bringing all of its properties into the UK tax net for capital gains purposes, etc.

This can be very difficult (and costly) to achieve in practice and detailed professional advice should always be sought before attempting to rely on this strategy.

Non-UK Resident Individuals

By using a UK Resident company, a non-UK resident individual property investor would effectively be bringing properties into the UK tax net.

As explained in section 3.4, however, there are some instances where this may still be a sensible strategy, taking the overall situation into account.

Furthermore, since the income from UK properties is always taxable in any case, the use of a UK company may often remain advantageous.

However, the major drawback for a non-resident in using a UK company is the fact that the company will be subject to UK tax (Corporation Tax) on its capital gains, whereas the individual would not be.

The only way to avoid any tax on the properties' capital growth in the company would be for the non-Resident individual to sell the company itself, rather than the properties held within it. Nevertheless, even then, one might reasonably expect the purchaser to take the potential Corporation Tax liability on capital gains in the company into account when negotiating a purchase price! (Although, against this, there are also Stamp Duty advantages to be considered, as explained in section 14.3.)

Chapter 15

Weighing It All Up

Now that we have carried out a detailed examination of the tax implications of using a property company, what conclusions can we draw?

1. A property company's usefulness will depend on the type of property business that you have. Property development, trading and management businesses will all generally benefit from being carried out through a company. The position for property investment businesses, where long-term capital growth tends to be an integral part of the business plan, is less clear.

2. A company will usually save you tax on your annual income.

3. The tax saving on income will, however, only be marginal (and will sometimes be eliminated) when profits are always being withdrawn from the company.

4. Greater savings result where the company's profits are being continually reinvested. This, in turn, leads to a significant growth in pre-tax income and the total capital value of the company.

5. Capital and income growth can be greatly accelerated by 'gearing up' the reinvestment of the company's retained after-tax profits through the use of borrowings to enhance the amount of capital available for investment.

6. Greater tax liabilities will arise on property disposals if the investor wishes to extract the proceeds from the company.

7. Capital growth retained in the company, however, may ultimately be sold at a lesser tax cost.

8. A successful property company is attractive to purchasers.

9. Properties held in companies should not be used privately.

10. Transferring existing investment properties into a company is extremely hazardous!

11. Property management companies may be considered as an alternative to property investment companies in the right circumstances.

12. Commercial investment properties will probably be better left out of a company.

13. Non-residents and those intending to emigrate should generally not use UK companies.

14. To be certain about the benefits of a property company requires a crystal ball.

15. The decision whether to use a company is dependent on a great many factors and each property investor's position is unique.

Happy (House) Hunting!

Chapter 16

Future Tax Changes

On 10th December 2003, Gordon Brown, the Chancellor of the Exchequer, included the following statement in his Pre-Budget report:

> "The Government is concerned that the longstanding differences in tax treatment between earned income and dividend income should not distort business strategies, or enable reductions by tax planning of individuals' tax liability."

He went on to state that, as a result of this "concern", he was planning to introduce new rules in his 2004 Budget to

> "ensure that the right amount of tax is paid by owner managers of small incorporated businesses on the profits extracted from their company."

These statements went on to be given the nickname of 'IR591' in professional tax circles and they caused a great deal of consternation.

The hot favourite amongst most commentators was the possibility that National Insurance Contributions would be introduced on dividends paid to owner-managers out of their own companies. This would have proved to be a major blow to countless small companies in the UK.

Thankfully, as it has transpired, the change highlighted in section 2.3 is far less draconian, as is illustrated by the fact that the only change to my conclusions in chapter fifteen was to insert '(and will sometimes be eliminated)' in point 3.

So, Are We Out Of The Woods Then?

Unfortunately not, since, once again, the Chancellor included a small, but nonetheless vital, comment, buried deep within his Budget press notices, as follows:

> "To ensure that targeted tax incentives support the Government's objectives for growth, enterprise and productivity, the Government proposes to consider the issues raised by the interaction with the tax system of definitions of income of self-employment, and the remuneration paid to owner managers, in a discussion paper which will be issued at the time of the 2004 Pre-Budget Report."

This piece of legalistic gobbledegook may well mean that further unpleasant changes for small companies are still on the way.

What it looks like to me, in fact, is that the Government has so far found it too difficult to come up with the necessary draft legislation to do what they really want to do, and has settled for the new Corporation Tax charge on small company dividends in the meantime.

Hence, National Insurance Contributions on small company dividends might still be on their way in, say, 2005 or, more likely, 2006. However, if such a tax were introduced:

- Would it be on all small company dividends, or only some of them?
- How would a 'small company' be defined?
- Would it be possible to escape any new tax charge by ensuring that you pay yourself a reasonable level of salary in the first place?
- Would it affect property businesses, where, after all, National Insurance Contributions aren't payable on the income in the first place?
- Will it matter whether the owner of the company is over retirement age and hence wouldn't normally be liable for National Insurance Contributions?

How Does this Affect the Decision on Whether to Use a Company?

From what we can tell so far, it does not look as if there will be a further attack on the Corporation Tax regime itself, but only on the extraction of profits by owner-managers.

As we have already seen in the previous chapters of this guide, a company is generally not very beneficial where all of its profits are being extracted by the owner every year. Hence, any changes we are likely to see in Budget 2005 or Budget 2006 will simply reinforce this conclusion.

It should, in the author's view, remain safe to say that a company is a useful vehicle through which to make long-term property investments and to build up a property portfolio over a number of years. The existing drawbacks to profit extraction will remain and may worsen to some degree.

The problems of corporate capital gains will remain and, one would hope, should not be exacerbated by any future changes.

In general, what the threatened changes probably mean from a tax-planning perspective is that those whose position is currently borderline should hold off from moving into a property company until the exact nature of any new regime is known.

Where, however, as in many cases, the argument in favour of a company is currently overwhelmingly favourable, this is likely to remain the case, although the Treasury can be expected to eat into your tax savings to some extent.

Appendix A

Corporation Tax Calculations: The 'Official' Format

As explained in section 2.2, when you see a Corporation Tax calculation which has been produced by the Inland Revenue, or by most accounting software, it will appear in the 'official' format and will not make any mention of marginal rates.

For the 'official' format, the company is taxed only at the following rates (subject, as always, to whether it has any associated companies, and to the possible additional charge on distributed profits):

- Total profits* up to £10,000:
  Zero

- Total profits* over £10,000, but no more than £300,000:
  19%

- Total profits* over £300,000:
  30%

* - 'profits' for this purpose include capital gains and UK dividend income (see below).

Where, however, total profits (including capital gains and UK dividend income) fall in either the range £10,000 to £50,000 or the range £300,000 to £1,500,000, the company will be entitled to marginal relief.

We will return to our example to see how this works in practice.

Example

Aaron Limited makes a total taxable profit of £400,000 for the year ended 31st December 2004. The company's Corporation Tax liability calculated under the 'official' format looks like this:

	£
£400,000 @ 30% =	*120,000*
Less marginal relief:	
(£1,500,000 - £400,000) x 11/400 =	*(30,250)*
Corporation Tax payable:	*89,750*

As you can see, this produces exactly the same result, only it's just a lot harder to understand!

UK Dividend Income

UK companies do not pay tax on dividends received from other UK companies but, if these are not from members of the same Group, the income has to be counted when looking at the Corporation Tax rates applicable to the recipient company's taxable income.

To illustrate this, we will return to Aaron Limited.

Example Revisited

In addition to its taxable profit of £400,000 for the year ended 31st December 2004, Aaron Limited also received UK dividends of £9,000 from unconnected companies.

Although the amount of taxable profit remains £400,000, the company's Corporation Tax liability has to be calculated on the basis of total income of £410,000 for marginal relief purposes (£400,000 plus the £9,000 of dividend income plus £1,000 for the tax credit on that dividend income at the rate of $1/9^{th}$).

	£
£400,000 @ 30% =	120,000
(Unchanged)	
Less marginal relief:	
(£1,500,000 - £410,000) x 11/400 =	(29,975)
Corporation Tax payable:	90,025

As you can see, the so-called 'tax-free' income of £9,000 has caused a £275 increase in the company's Corporation Tax bill. Not much, but hardly 'tax-free' either!

Appendix B

Connected Persons

Connected persons include:

- Husband or wife

- Mother, father or remoter ancestor

- Son, daughter or remoter descendant

- Brother or sister

- Mother-in-law, father-in-law, son-in-law, daughter-in-law, brother-in-law or sister-in-law

- Business partners

- Companies under the control of the other party to the transaction or of any of his/her relatives, as above

- Trustees of a trust where the other party to the transaction, or any of his/her relatives as above, is a beneficiary.

Appendix C

Tax Rates and Allowances
2002/2003 to 2004/2005

	Rates	Bands, allowances, etc.		
		2002/2003 £	2003/2004 £	2004/2005 £
Income tax				
Personal allowance		4,615	4,615	4,745
Starting rate	10%	1,920	1,960	2,020
Basic rate	22%	27,980	28,540	29,380
Higher rate on over	40%	29,900	30,500	31,400
Children's Tax Credit	10%	5,290	Revised*	Revised*
Baby Tax Credit	10%	10,490	Revised*	Revised*
Pension scheme earnings cap		97,200	99,000	102,000
Capital Gains Tax				
Annual exemption:				
Individuals		7,700	7,900	8,200
Trusts		3,850	3,950	4,100
Inheritance Tax				
Nil Rate Band Threshold		250,000	255,000	263,000
Pensioners, etc.				
Age allowance: 65 –74		6,100	6,610	6,830
Age allowance: 75 & over		6,370	6,720	6,950
MCA: born before 6/4/35		5,465	5,565	5,725
MCA: 75 & over		5,535	5,635	5,795
MCA minimum		2,110	2,150	2,210
Income limit		17,900	18,300	18,900
Blind Person's Allowance		1,480	1,510	1,560

* - Replaced by Working Tax Credit and Child Tax Credit, with effect from 6th April 2003.

Appendix D

More Complex Corporation Tax Calculations

D.1 When Tax Rates Change

Where a company draws up accounts for a period that straddles any date on which the Corporation Tax rates have been changed, its profits and gains are apportioned on a time basis between the pre-change period and the post-change period.

Most recently, of course, this will apply to any accounting periods that straddle 1st April 2002.

Example
Twickenham Limited made profits of £200,000 for the year ended 30th June 2002. Nine months of the year precede 1st April 2002 and hence 9/12ths of the profit is taxed at the old Small Companies Rate of 20%:

$$9/12 \times £200,000 = £150,000 @ 20\% = £30,000$$

The final three months of the accounting period fall on/after 1st April 2002 and hence the remainder of the profit is taxed at the new Small Companies Rate of 19%:

3/12 x £200,000 = £50,000 @ 19% = £9,500

Total Corporation Tax due = £39,500 (giving an overall effective rate of 19.75%)

D.2 Shorter or Longer Accounting Periods

For a variety of reasons, companies sometimes prepare accounts covering periods other than a year. This happens most often at the beginning or end of a company's life, although it will also occur in the event of a change of accounting date. (We saw one of the reasons why you might wish to consider changing your company's accounting date in section 2.4.)

As shorter or longer accounting periods will often occur at the beginning of a company's life, it is worth us spending a little time on the Corporation Tax implications of such periods in this Appendix.

Longer Accounting Periods

For Corporation Tax purposes, periods of over one year must be divided up into two periods:

- The first twelve months, and

- The remainder.

Each of these periods is then taxed separately in its own right. The first period is taxed under the normal principles applying to a period of a year. The second period is dealt with as a short accounting period.

Short Accounting Periods

Where a company has a short accounting period, all of the profit bands and limits set out above must be reduced accordingly.

Example
Lansdowne Road Limited draws up accounts for the period ended 31st March 2003, showing a profit of £48,000.

If this were the profit of a 12-month period, the Corporation Tax payable would be:

£10,000 @ 0% = £0

£38,00 @23.75% = £9,025
Total tax due = £9,025

However, if this were a nine-month period, the Corporation Tax calculation would be as follows:

£7,500 (£10,000 x 9 /12) @ 0%   = £0
£30,000 (£40,000 x 9 /12) @ 23.75% = £7,125
£10,500 (Remainder)   @ 19%   = £1,995

Total Tax Due: £9,120

Simple method: £48,000   @ 19.00% = £9,120

The 'Simple Method' applies here despite the fact that Lansdowne Road Limited's profits are below the £50,000 limit at which the Small Companies Rate (19%) usually begins to apply. Because of the company's shorter accounting period, this limit is effectively reduced to £37,500 (£50,000 x 9/12).

Appendix E

Paying Corporation Tax

For most companies, payment of Corporation Tax is due in one single lump sum payable by the date falling nine months and one day after the end of the accounting period.

For example, the Corporation Tax for the year ended 31st December 2004 will be due by 1st October 2005.

As usual, interest is charged on late payments. The rate is varied in line with commercial interest rates. Changes in the rate are announced via Inland Revenue Press Releases as they come into force and are generally designed to keep the rate for interest on overdue Corporation Tax at around 2.5% above base rate.

Unlike Income Tax, interest on overdue Corporation Tax is now a deductible expense for Corporation Tax purposes. The reason for this is that, with the introduction of Corporation Tax Self Assessment for accounting periods ending on or after 1st July 1999, it was decided that the Inland Revenue's interest charges on companies should be more in line with interest rates on commercial debt.

E.1 Long Accounting Periods

Where a company has a long accounting period, in excess of a year, then, as explained in Appendix D, this will be treated for Corporation Tax purposes as two periods, namely:

- The first 12 months, and

- The remainder.

In these cases, the Corporation Tax payable in respect of each period will be due nine months and a day after that period ends.

Example

Square Peg Limited draws up accounts for the 15-month period ended 30th September 2004. The company must therefore calculate its Corporation Tax separately for the period of twelve months ended 30th June 2004 and for the period of three months ended 30th September 2004.

The Corporation Tax for the year ended 30th June 2004 will be due by 1st April 2005.

The Corporation Tax for the three months to 30th September 2004 will be due by 1st July 2005.

Generally speaking, the Inland Revenue will send the company a payslip about a month before the Corporation Tax is due, to enable it to make its payment on time. (Payment of the tax, however, remains the company's responsibility and the Inland Revenue will not be interested in any excuses revolving around the fact that the company did not receive a payslip from them in time!)

E.2 Large Companies

Those companies that are large enough, or profitable enough (or, perhaps even stupid enough, as discussed in section 14.4), to be paying Corporation Tax at the main rate of 30% are now subject to an instalment system.

Broadly, in most cases, the large company instalment system requires such companies to pay their Corporation Tax in quarterly instalments, commencing six months and 13 days after the first day of the accounting period. Naturally, this means that large companies need to estimate their tax liabilities in advance.

As you might expect, the Inland Revenue imposes interest charges for any resultant underpayments. Fortunately, however, a lower rate of interest applies to late payments under the instalment system. The usual full rate of interest is imposed once more in the case of any Corporation Tax still unpaid nine months after the end of the relevant period.

Appendix F
Company Tax Returns

For accounting periods ending on or after 1st July 1999, companies now also fall under a Self-Assessment system (which replaced the 'Pay and File' system for Corporation Tax). The corporate system is referred to as Corporation Tax Self Assessment or CTSA for short.

F.1 Filing Deadlines

Under Corporation Tax Self Assessment, the company is generally required to submit a Tax Return within 12 months of its accounting date.

However, an exception to this rule may occur in some instances. The actual rule (other than in the case of long accounting periods – see below) is that the company must file its Return by the later of:

a) Twelve months from the end of its accounting period, or

b) Three months from the date on which the notice requiring the company to deliver a Tax Return for the period was served by the Inland Revenue.

In the context of (b) above, however, readers should note that there are penalties for failing to notify the Inland Revenue of the company's chargeability to Corporation Tax (see section F.5). Hence, it generally requires a bit of 'good luck' for the company to be able to get a later filing date under this rule. It does happen though:

Example
Adam Smith Properties Limited was set up on 1st July 2003 and draws up its first set of accounts for the year ended 30th June 2004. The company duly completed and submitted a form CT41G in August 2003.

On 31st May 2005, the company still hasn't received a notice requiring it to deliver a Tax Return from the Inland Revenue.

Hence, on 4ᵗʰ June 2005, the Company Secretary writes to the local Tax Office and advises them of the company's chargeability to Corporation Tax for the year ended 30ᵗʰ June 2004.

On 28ᵗʰ June 2005, the Inland Revenue finally serves a notice requiring the company to deliver a Tax Return.

The company must therefore file its Tax Return by the earlier of:

   a) *Twelve months after its accounting date – i.e. 30ᵗʰ June 2005, or*
   b) *Three months from the date of the notice - i.e. 28ᵗʰ September 2005.*

Hence, in this case, the Tax Return should be filed by 28ᵗʰ September 2005, almost 15 months after the end of the accounting period.

Unfortunately, in practice, the Inland Revenue are generally more 'on the ball' than this and will usually have issued a notice requiring the company to deliver a Tax Return in plenty of time to ensure that the usual 12-month deadline will apply. In other words, it is pretty rare for the Inland Revenue not to have issued the relevant notice more than three months before the end of the company's accounting period.

Companies House sends details of all new companies directly to the Inland Revenue shortly after they are formed. This generally enables the Inland Revenue to ensure that every company is brought into the Corporation Tax Self Assessment system as speedily as possible and its first Tax Return is therefore filed by the usual deadline.

F.2 Longer Accounting Periods

As usual, longer accounting periods (i.e. over a year) give rise to a few complications.

Firstly, two separate Corporation Tax Self Assessment Returns are required:

- One for the first 12 months of the accounting period, and

- One for the remainder of the accounting period.

Secondly, the date by which these Tax Returns are due will depend on the length of the accounting period:

- For accounting periods up to 18 months in length, both returns are due within 12 months of the accounting date.

- For accounting periods of more than 18 months in length, both returns are due within 30 months of the beginning of the accounting period.

Example 1

Springboks Limited draws up accounts for the 18-month period ended 30th November 2004. The company must therefore file two tax returns in respect of this accounting period:

- *One for the period of twelve months ended 31st May 2004, and*

- *One for the period of six months ended 30th November 2004.*

Both returns are due for filing with the Inland Revenue by 30th November 2005.

Example 2

Wallabies Limited draws up accounts for the 20-month period ended 31st March 2005. Again, the company must file two Tax Returns in respect of this accounting period. In this case, these are:

- *One for the period of twelve months ended 31st July 2004, and*

- *One for the period of eight months ended 31st March 2005.*

Both Returns are due for filing with the Inland Revenue within 30 months of the beginning of the accounting period on 1st August 2003, i.e. by 31st January 2006.

Wealth Warning

The date on which the Tax Return is due is determined quite independently of the date on which the payment of Corporation Tax is due. None of the above rules regarding filing deadlines has any impact on the date that payment is due, which generally remains nine months and a day after the end of the relevant period (except for large companies) as set out in section E.2.

Hence, in practice, whenever the rules give rise to later filing deadlines, it is of little real value since the company must still calculate and pay its Corporation Tax within the usual timescale.

F.3 Getting Notices Issued for the 'Right' Period

As a general rule, I would usually advise all company taxpayers to keep the taxman well informed of any changes that affect the company's Tax Return periods, including any changes of accounting date, the setting up of new companies and commencement of business. ('Starting up' type issues are covered further in section 11.2 in the main body of the guide.)

In this way, one hopes that the Inland Revenue will issue notices requiring the company to deliver Tax Returns for the right periods. Believe me, there is generally nothing to be gained by trying to be clever and allowing the Inland Revenue to issue notices for the wrong periods!

Wealth Warning

Most important of all is to advise the Inland Revenue if the company ceases all business activity and becomes inactive. Such a company is usually known as a 'dormant' company.

A dormant company should not have to file a Tax Return, but may still have to do so if a notice requiring the company to deliver a Tax Return has already been issued by the Inland Revenue. Where a Tax Return remains due, penalties may still arise (see section F.5).

Note that the receipt of any form of taxable income, or capital gains, by the company, including the mere receipt of bank interest on a small deposit (no matter how small), will mean that the company remains within the charge to Corporation Tax and must therefore still file a Tax Return for the period.

Tax Tip

Although, strictly speaking, a Tax Return will be due if a Corporation Tax Self Assessment notice has been issued in respect of a period, the Inland Revenue will sometimes be prepared to withdraw the notice without penalty if the company is genuinely dormant throughout the period.

In such cases, it is best to contact the Inland Revenue as early as possible to explain the situation. If this is done, they will often be happy to withdraw the notice. After all, it saves them a lot of time and effort too!

But what if a Notice is Issued for the Wrong Period?

If the Inland Revenue issues a notice requiring the company to deliver a Tax Return for a period that does not correspond with the company's accounting period, the following rules apply:

i) The company must file Tax Returns for any accounting periods that end during, or at the end of, the period specified in the notice. This will include cases where two Tax Returns are required for an accounting period (i.e. longer accounting periods).

Example
Eagles Limited prepared accounts for the year ended 31st December 2004 and then for the six months ended 30th June 2005.

The Inland Revenue issues a notice requiring Eagles Limited to submit a Tax Return for the period 1st July 2004 to 30th June 2005.

Eagles Limited must submit Tax Returns for the year ended 31st December 2004 and for the six months *ended 30th June 2005 in order to comply with this notice.*

ii) If no accounting periods of the company end during, or at the end of, the period specified in the notice, but an accounting period does begin during that period, then the company must file a Tax Return for the part of the notice period that precedes that accounting period.

Example

Pumas Limited was incorporated on 11th October 2003. It commenced business on 1st January 2004 and prepared accounts for the year ended 31st December 2004.

The Inland Revenue issues a notice requiring Pumas Limited to submit a Tax Return for the period 11th October 2003 to 10th October 2004.

Pumas Limited must submit a Tax Return for the period from 11th October to 31st December 2003 in order to comply with this notice.

(NB: This Tax Return is due by 31st December 2004, or three months after the issue of the relevant notice, if later.)

iii) If the company was outside the charge to Corporation Tax for the whole of the period specified in the notice, a Tax Return is required for the whole of that period.

Example

Sweet Chariot Limited has been dormant for many years and prepares dormant company accounts to 31st March each year.

Suspecting that Sweet Chariot Limited may no longer be dormant, the Inland Revenue issues a notice requiring the company to submit a Tax Return for the period 23rd November 2002 to 22nd November 2003.

Despite the fact that Sweet Chariot Limited draws up accounts to 31st March, it will need to submit a Tax Return for the year ended 22nd November 2003 in order to comply with this notice.

(NB: See section F.5 for the possible penalties that might arise if the Inland Revenue's suspicions prove to be well-founded.)

iv) If none of the above applies, the notice is ineffective and there is no requirement to submit a Tax Return in response to *that* notice. Remember, though, that the company is still required to notify the Inland Revenue of the company's chargeability to Corporation Tax for any period for which it does not receive a valid notice.

Example

Famous Grouse Limited draws up accounts for the year ended 31st December 2004.

The Inland Revenue issues a notice requiring Famous Grouse Limited to deliver a Tax Return for the period 1st April to 30th September 2004.

As no accounting period of the company either begins or ends within the period specified in the notice, the notice is ineffective.

If no valid notice for the period is issued, Famous Grouse Limited must notify the Inland Revenue of its chargeability to Corporation Tax for this period by 31st December 2005 in order to avoid any risk of a penalty.

F.4 The Tax Return

The Corporation Tax Self Assessment Tax Return document is called a CT600. At 12 pages, the basic CT600 Return is only two pages longer than the Tax Return for individuals.

However, with its Corporation Tax Self Assessment Tax Return, the company is also required to submit:

- Its statutory accounts (small and medium-sized companies who are permitted to file abbreviated accounts with Companies House must nevertheless still submit a full set of accounts to the Inland Revenue with their Tax Return).

- A Corporation Tax computation (i.e. a calculation of the amount of profits and gains chargeable to Corporation Tax for the accounting period).

- A Corporation Tax Self-Assessment (i.e. a calculation of the amount of Corporation Tax due).

These last two items can generally be prepared as a single combined calculation and there is plenty of accountancy software available to produce this.

Additionally, rather like the individual Self Assessment Return, there are 'supplementary pages' which must also be submitted in a number of cases, including:

- CT600A: Loans to participators by close companies.
- CT600B: Controlled foreign companies.
- CT600C: Group and consortium relief claims or surrender.
- CT600D: Extra details for some insurance companies.
- CT600E: Charities – where full or partial exemption from tax is being claimed.
- CT600F: Tonnage tax.
- CT600G: Corporate venturing.

Of these, most property companies are only ever likely to be concerned with the CT600A supplement, which covers 'loans to participators'. These arise whenever a shareholder or director of a close company owes money to that company. A temporary tax charge arises in such cases, which is repayable when the debt to the company is itself repaid.

Group and consortium relief claims, which are dealt with on the CT600C supplement, may arise where the company is either part of a group of companies (i.e. group relief) or is owned by, or is a member of, a corporate consortium (i.e. consortium relief). In such cases, and in the right circumstances, one company may claim to offset the losses of another company against its profits or gains, as long as the other company agrees to 'surrender' those losses.

Group or consortium relief will not affect many property companies and we saw in section 14.4 that the formation of a group of companies can have unintended adverse consequences. Nevertheless, there may be circumstances where a group is desirable.

Documentation and Extra Help

Usually, the company will be issued with a CT600 for each accounting period, together with any supplementary pages which the Inland Revenue are already aware will be required. The Inland Revenue will usually also issue the company with a CT600 guide, which contains notes on how to calculate certain items (such as turnover, for example).

The CT600, the guide, and any supplementary pages can also be obtained by calling the Corporation Tax Self Assessment Orderline on 0845 300 6555, or via the Internet at www.inlandrevenue.gov.uk

F.5 Penalties

Naturally, as one would expect, the Corporation Tax Self Assessment regime includes penalties for late Tax Returns, as well as sundry other 'transgressions'. The main items to be aware of are set out below.

In general terms, it is fair to make the point that the corporate regime has a few more 'teeth' and is a little stricter on those who do not quite meet its rigorous requirements. This, perhaps, is the price we must pay for more beneficial tax rates.

Having said that, I have always found that Companies House, in particular, has generally been very understanding with new company owners.

Late Returns

There is a progressive system of penalties for late Tax Returns under Corporation Tax Self Assessment, as follows:

i) Returns filed up to three months late incur a fixed-flat rate penalty of £100.

ii) Returns filed more than three months late incur a fixed flat-rate penalty of £200.

iii) The amounts at (i) and (ii) above are increased to £500 and £1,000 respectively in the case of a third, or subsequent, successive failure. A 'failure' for this purpose means any late submission, not necessarily a 'failure' to the same degree as applies in that third successive year.

The increased penalties do not apply, however, if the company is outside the charge to Corporation Tax at any time within the three relevant successive periods.

Example 1
Les Bleu Limited draws up accounts to 31st March each year.

The company submits its Tax Return for the year ended 31st March 2003 one day late, on 1st April 2004. A £100 penalty arises.

Its Tax Return for the year ended 31st March 2004 is again submitted one day late, on 1st April 2005. Another £100 penalty arises.

The Tax Return for the year ended 31st March 2005 is submitted over three months late, on 15th July 2006. This is the third consecutive failure and the penalty arising is therefore £1,000.

Example 2
Red Dragons Limited draws up accounts to 31st December each year.

The company's Tax Returns for the periods ended 31st December 2003, 2004 and 2005 are all submitted more than three months late. Penalties of £200 have been *incurred in respect of the first two of these periods. Initially, it looks like a £1,000 penalty will arise for the third period.*

However, Red Dragons Limited is able to point out that the company had, in fact, ceased all business activity altogether for the first three months of 2004. Serious consideration had been given to winding the company up, but, in the end, business activity had resumed on 1st April 2004, with accounts drawn up to 31st December 2004 representing nine months of trading.

Hence, although Red Dragons Limited will still be liable for a £200 late filing penalty in respect of their Tax Return for the year ended 31st December 2004, this will not be increased to £1,000 as the company had not remained within the charge to Corporation Tax throughout the whole of the three successive accounting periods then ended.

Wealth Warning

Although there may in some cases be a reduction (or, more properly, <u>not</u> be an increase) in the fixed flat rate penalty where the company has not continuously remained within the charge to Corporation Tax, it should be noted that these penalties are applied regardless of whether the company does, in fact, have any Corporation Tax liability for the period.

This is unlike the position under Self Assessment for individuals, where there is no late filing penalty if no actual tax liability arises. Property investors who begin to operate through a company should bear this point in mind!

iv) In addition to the fixed penalties under (i) to (iii) above, the company is also liable for a 'tax-geared' penalty of 10% if it fails to file a Corporation Tax Self Assessment Tax Return within 18 months after the end of the period to which the Return relates.

The penalty of 10% is applied by reference to any 'unpaid Tax'. 'Unpaid tax' means the amount of Corporation Tax payable for the period which remains unpaid on the date on which the liability to the penalty arises.

Example

Azurri Limited draws up accounts for the year ended 31st December 2003. Due to a number of problems with the business, the accounts are not completed until 2005, meaning that the Tax Return is very late.

On 20th June 2005, the company makes an estimated Corporation Tax payment of £6,000.

Later, in August 2005, the company makes a further Corporation Tax payment of £1,000 in respect of the period.

In September 2005, the accounts are finally completed. The Tax Return is submitted on 1st October 2005, showing a final Corporation Tax liability of £9,500.

A Tax-Geared penalty arises on 30th June 2005, 18 months after the end of Azurri Limited's accounting period. The amount of unpaid tax for the period at that date is £3,500 (£9,500 less £6,000). The Tax-Geared penalty arising is therefore £350 (10% x £3,500).

Note that the payment made in June 2005, i.e. within 18 months of the accounting period, may be taken into account in determining the amount of 'unpaid tax', but the payment made in August 2005 is of no effect for this purpose.

(The company will also have a fixed flat-rate penalty of £200, or £1,000 if this is its third successive failure.)

v) The 'Tax-Geared' penalty increases to 20% if the Tax Return is filed more than two years after the end of the relevant period. In effect, this will be calculated as a further 10% on any tax still remaining unpaid two years after the end of the relevant period.

Example Revisited

Returning to Azurri Limited, in the example above, let us suppose that the facts remain the same except that the Tax Return is not filed until January 2006, i.e. more than two years after the end of the accounting period.

The unpaid tax after 18 months remains £3,500, giving rise to a penalty of £350, as above. However, the amount unpaid after two years is reduced, by the second payment made in August 2005, to £2,500. The additional penalty arising at this date is therefore £250 (10% again), making a total Tax-Geared penalty of £600.

(This may alternatively be arrived at as 20% of the tax unpaid after two years (20% x £2,500 = £500) plus an additional 10% on the further amount which had been unpaid after 18 months, but which was paid within the two-year period (10% x £1,000 = £100). Total penalty = £500 + £100 = £600.)

Wealth Warning

It is important to note that the 'tax-geared' penalties under (iv) and (v) above arise by reference to the end of the period for which the Tax Return is made up and not by reference to the filing deadline.

Example

Wood & Co. Limited drew up accounts for the six months ended 30th November 2004.

Despite having advised the Inland Revenue of its chargeability to Corporation Tax for the period, the company did not receive a notice requiring it to deliver a Tax Return for this period until 15th February 2006. The Tax Return was therefore not actually due until 15th May 2006.

However, despite this late filing deadline, Wood & Co, Limited, will be subject to a penalty of 10% of any unpaid tax if its Tax Return is not submitted to the Inland Revenue by 31st May 2006. (Or 20% if not submitted by 30th November 2006.)

There is no liability to the fixed rate penalties at (i) to (iii) above if the company has obtained an extension to the filing date by which it must file its accounts at Companies House from the Registrar of Companies and it files its Corporation Tax Self Assessment Tax Return with the Inland Revenue within that same extended deadline. Note that this has no effect on the 'Tax-Geared' penalties under (iv) and (v) above.

Determinations

If the company's Corporation Tax Self Assessment Tax Return is overdue, the Inland Revenue may issue a determination. This is effectively an Inland Revenue estimate of the Corporation Tax due and enables them to commence collection proceedings. Penalties will also be raised and collected in line with the amount of Corporation Tax due according to the determination.

A determination may be superseded by the submission of a completed Tax Return by the later of:

- Twelve months from the date of the determination, or

- Five years from the original filing date.

Failure to Notify Chargeability

As explained previously, a company has a duty to notify the Inland Revenue of its chargeability to Corporation Tax for any accounting period for which it is within the charge to Corporation Tax and does not receive a valid notice requiring it to deliver a Tax Return.

The notification of chargeability must reach the Inland Revenue within 12 months from the end of the accounting period concerned.

The penalty for failing to notify the Inland Revenue in time may not exceed the amount of unpaid tax for the period on the date that the 12-month notice period expires.

In other words, the Inland Revenue may impose a penalty up to an amount equal to the Corporation Tax which is not paid within 12 months of the end of the accounting period.

In practice, of course, the duty to notify is usually satisfied by submitting a Tax Return by the date on which it would have been due had a notice been issued on time. (Although care needs to be taken in the case of long accounting periods.)

Furthermore, no penalty can arise under this provision if the correct amount of Corporation Tax has been paid by the normal due date.

Fraudulent or Negligent Returns

Penalties are due where a company fraudulently or negligently files an incorrect Tax Return. This also covers the case where an innocent error is later discovered by the company and not rectified without unreasonable delay.

In practice, the amounts of penalties charged under these provisions will depend on the seriousness of the offence. In the most serious cases, the Inland Revenue will bring criminal proceedings against the directors of the company and any other persons found to be responsible for the fraudulent Returns.

Tax Tip

Where genuine doubts exist over the correct treatment for Corporation Tax purposes of any item in the company's accounts, the best course of action is to ensure that the matter is fully disclosed to the Inland Revenue on the face of the Tax Return.

The Inland Revenue may not agree with your treatment of the item, but would be unable to assert that there had been any fraudulent behaviour on the part of the company, its directors or its advisers.

This approach is only valid in genuinely doubtful cases. If the correct treatment of an item is clear, then that correct treatment must be followed regardless of any additional disclosure.

Need Affordable & Expert Tax Planning Advice?

Try Our Unique Question & Answer Service

The purpose of this guide is to provide you with detailed guidance on the pros and cons of using a company to invest in property.

Ultimately you may want to take further action or obtain advice personal to your circumstances.

Taxcafe.co.uk has a unique online tax advice service that provides access to highly qualified tax professionals at an affordable rate.

No matter how complex your question, we will provide you with detailed tax planning guidance through this service. The cost is just £69.95.

To find out more go to **www.taxcafe.co.uk** and click the Tax Questions button.

Pay Less Tax!

... with help from Taxcafe's unique tax guides, software and Q&A service

All products available online at **www.taxcafe.co.uk**

➤ **How to Avoid Property Tax.** Essential reading for property investors who want to know all the tips and tricks to follow to pay less tax on their property profits.

➤ **Using a Property Company to Save Tax.** How to massively increase your profits by using a property company... plus all the traps to avoid.

➤ **How to Avoid Inheritance Tax**. A-Z of Inheritance Tax planning, with clear explanations & numerous examples. Covers simple & sophisticated tax planning.

➤ **Non Resident & Offshore Tax Planning**. How to exploit non-resident tax status to reduce your tax bill, plus advice on using offshore trusts and companies.

➤ **Incorporate & Save Tax**. Everything you need to know about the tax benefits of using a company to run your business.

➤ **Bonus vs Dividends.** Shows how shareholder/directors of companies can save thousands in tax by choosing the optimal mix of bonus and dividends.

➤ **Selling a Business.** A potential minefield with numerous traps to avoid but significant tax saving opportunities.

➢ **How to Claim Tax Credits.** Even families with higher incomes can make successful tax credit claims. This guide shows how much you can claim and how to go about it.

➢ **Property Capital Gains Tax Calculator.** Unique software that performs complex Capital Gains Tax calculations in seconds.

➢ **Fast Tax Advice**. We offer a unique Tax Question Service. Answers from highly qualified specialist tax advisers. Just click the Tax Questions button on our site.

Essential Property Investment Guides

...written by leading experts and packed with tips & tricks of the trade

All products available online at www.taxcafe.co.uk

- ➢ **An Insider's Guide to Successful Property Investing.** Little-known secrets of successful property investors. A "must read" for anyone interested in making big profits and avoiding costly mistakes.

- ➢ **An Insider's Guide to Successful Property Investing - Part II.** How the experts make millions by using simple but clever techniques to find, buy, manage and sell property.

- ➢ **No Money Down Property Millions.** Written by a wealthy property investor, this entertaining and brilliantly clever guide shows you how to invest in property without using any of your own money.

- ➢ **The Successful Landlord's Handbook.** Definitive guide for Buy to Let investors. Covers: sourcing cheap property, using borrowed money to earn big capital gains, finding quality tenants, earning high rents, legal traps, letting agents, and lots more...

- ➢ **63 Common Defects in Investment Property & How to Spot Them.** With full colour illustrations, this unique guide will save you thousands by steering you clear of no-hope property investments and towards bargain-priced gems.

- ➢ **Property Auctions Bargains.** One of the best-kept secrets of successful property investors is to buy at rock-bottom prices at auction. This A-Z guide tells you everything you need to know.

www.taxcafe.co.uk

DISCLAIMER BY TAXCAFE UK LIMITED

1. Please note that this Tax Guide is intended as general guidance only for individual readers and does NOT constitute accountancy, tax, investment or other professional advice. Further general tax guidance on circumstances not covered in this Tax Guide can be obtained through the TAXCafe™ online "Question and Answer Service which is available at www.taxcafe.co.uk. Taxcafe UK Limited accepts no responsibility or liability for loss which may arise from reliance on information contained in this Tax Guide.

2. Please note that tax legislation, the law and practices by government and regulatory authorities (e.g. the Inland Revenue) are constantly changing and the information contained in this Tax Guide is only correct as at the date of publication. We therefore recommend that for accountancy, tax, investment or other professional advice, you consult a suitably qualified accountant, tax specialist, independent financial adviser, or other professional adviser. Please also note that your personal circumstances may vary from the general examples given in this Tax Guide and your professional adviser will be able to give specific advice based on your personal circumstances.

3. This Tax Guide covers UK taxation only and any references to "tax" or "taxation" in this Tax Guide, unless the contrary is expressly stated, refers to UK taxation only. Please note that references to the "UK" do not include the Channel Islands or the Isle of Man. Foreign tax implications are beyond the scope of this Tax Guide.

4. Whilst in an effort to be helpful, this Tax Guide may refer to general guidance on matters other than UK taxation, Taxcafe UK Limited are not experts in these matters and do not accept any responsibility or liability for loss which may arise from reliance on such information contained in this Tax Guide.

5. Please note that Taxcafe UK Limited has relied wholly on the expertise of the author in the preparation of the content of this Tax Guide. The author is not an employee of Taxcafe UK Limited but has been selected by Taxcafe UK Limited using reasonable care and skill to write the content of this Tax Guide.

Printed in the United Kingdom
by Lightning Source UK Ltd.
100126UKS00001BB/1